the Groovy Chicks' Road Trip to Love

the Groovy Chicks' Road Trip to Love

Dena Dyer & Laurie Barker Copeland

Bringing Home the Message for Life

COOK COMMUNICATIONS MINISTRIES
Colorado Springs, Colorado • Paris, Ontario
KINGSWAY COMMUNICATIONS LTD
Eastbourne, England

Life Journey® is an imprint of
Cook Communications Ministries, Colorado Springs, CO 80918
Cook Communications, Paris, Ontario
Kingsway Communications, Eastbourne, England

THE GROOVY CHICKS' ROAD TRIP TO LOVE
© 2006 by Laurie Barker Copeland and Dena Dyer

The Web addresses (URLs) recommended throughout this book are solely
offered as a resource to the reader. The citation of these Web sites does
not in any way imply an endorsement on the part of the author or the
publisher, nor does the author or publisher vouch for their content for the
life of this book.

Cover Design and Photo Illustration: TrueBlue Design/Sandy Flewelling

First Printing, 2006
Printed in the United States of America

1 2 3 4 5 6 7 8 9 10 Printing/Year 11 10 09 08 07 06

ISBN-13: 978-0-7814-4353-1
ISBN-10: 0-7814-4353-9

LCCN: 2005939114

Contents

PART THREE
I WANNA HOLD YOUR HAND (YOUNG LOVE)

PART FOUR
GOIN' TO THE CHAPEL (MATURE LOVE)

PART FIVE
TIPTOE THROUGH THE TULIPS (CHILDREN'S LOVE)

Part Six
Nowhere to Run, Nowhere to Hide (God's Love)

ACKNOWLEDGMENTS

FROM LAURIE:

I am honored and humbled to have as part of my Groovy Chick family:

My faithful prayer warriors who almost daily walked (and prayed!) through this book with me: Linda Lee Jaunese, Christie Caldie, Janet Canon, Dean Crowe, Carole Suzanne Jackson, Kathy Carlton Willis, Olga Waters, Pat & Steve Ernst, Cathy Mitchell, Diane Terrell, Donna Funderburk, Laura Bridenbach, Lori Droppers, Mary Whitmore, Michelle Taylor, Rozie Hoebing, Sherry Everett, and Tami LaVoie.

My brainstorming buddies, with whom the ideas percolate: Cheri Cowell, Denise Modomo, Liz Collard, Tama Westman, and Debbie Smith.

My teachers who encourage this stumbling storyteller: Eva Marie Everson, the Word Weavers Group, Rhonda Rhea, Deb DiSandro, Florence Littauer, Marita Littauer, and CLASS.

My writing buddy and coauthor Dena Dyer: Hey Starshine, you know we fill in each other's gaps! I'm so glad you're on this breathtaking road trip with me. I'm having a blast!

My sweet, patient family: John, Kailey, Mom, Dad, Granny, Bill, Lois, Amy, Checker, Gloria, Michael, and Janna. From the days of fighting over backseat car space to making cranberry sauce, you've shown me how to love.

And to my God, Savior, and Lord ... I just flat out stand in amazement over the love you show me every day, everywhere.

DENA WANTS TO THANK:

Carey, Jordan, and Jackson—my three groovy dudes! Thanks for letting me follow God's call for my life, even though it means I'm sometimes unavailable. I couldn't do this without you! You are my most precious treasures, and I love you immeasurably.

My parents, who regularly encourage me with phone calls, cards, and prayers.

My brother, a groovy dude in every sense of the word. Thanks for being one of my biggest fans—and for bravely eating my cooking while we were growing up. I'm so sorry!

The Dyer family, who let me storm their gates on July 8, 1995, when I married Carey. (They've never been the same, bless their hearts.) Thanks for encouraging the two of us to follow our dreams, even when it meant we wouldn't live near you or get to see you that often. And thank you, Terry and Nancy, for being so generous, in every sense of the word. I love you dearly!

Laurie, my groovy partner in crime. It's been a real "trip" working with you—and I'm glad God brought us together. I can't wait to see what else He has in store ... thanks for spicing up my life, Pepper!

To my Lord and Savior, friend and counselor, Jesus Christ. I am in awe that you continue to use this earthen vessel. Thank you for healing me, strengthening me, and always showing up just when I need your mercy and peace. I am grateful beyond words—and I'll never quit singing your praises!

BOTH OF US WANT TO THANK:

Mary McNeil, our groovy editor. You saw the potential and "got" what we were trying to do from the beginning stages of the

Groovy Chicks. Thank you for your dedication, support, friendship, and sense of humor. You're definitely a chic Chick!

Michele Tennesen, Tom Beard, Diane Gardner, and the rest of the Cook Communications staff. We really appreciate your tireless work on our behalf. Stay groovy!

Frank Weimann, our agent at The Literary Group.

John Copeland, who besides being Laurie's hubby, is our super-talented Web designer (or Webrooster, as he likes to be called), sound guy, PowerPoint, video, and graphics guy (he came up with graphics for all the sidebars, as well as for the Groovy Chicks weekends we do). We pray we'll one day be able to pay you what you're worth. If not, we know you have a HUGE reward coming in heaven.

The many writers whose stories we couldn't accept. We genuinely appreciate your taking the time to submit your experiences. Sorry we couldn't use them all!

Our "Peeps"—the Groovy Chick contributors. Sing it with us, "We are family ... I got all my sisters with me." It's so fun to have such a great group of crazy, wonderful girlfriends on the road with us. You rock!

INTRODUCTION

Hey, can you roll up the car window so we can talk? Yeah, that's better!

Welcome to our second groovy road trip! We (along with our crazy alter egos Pepper and Starshine) are so happy you picked up this book. May these stories challenge, inspire, and encourage you in your own journey—the journey known as "life."

Our first *Groovy Chicks' Road Trip*™ volume was on peace. Now we're tackling another limitless subject—love. Yep, groovy love. But since "love" is so misrepresented and misunderstood in today's culture, let's see what one of our favorite authors has to say about the subject.

In his classic book *The Four Loves* (Harvest, 1971), C. S. Lewis makes the distinction between gift-love (which demands nothing in return and is closest to God himself) and the need-loves (earthly human loves, born out of our need to be loved). He then divides the need-loves into affection, friendship, and romantic love.

Lewis says that the three need-loves, when left to themselves, eventually go bad. They all need gift-love's input in order to thrive.

What kind of love do you think eight-year-old Rebecca is illustrating when she says, "When my grandmother got arthritis, she couldn't bend over and paint her toenails anymore. So my grandfather does it for her all the time, even when his hands got arthritis, too. That's love."

The wonderfully talented authors whose stories we've included in this volume recognize that God, through his son, Jesus Christ, is their source, goal, and guide. Whether their love stories are funny, poignant, sad, or miraculous, they have learned that experiencing (receiving and giving) love—in all its forms—can make us more like Jesus Christ.

Speaking of Jesus, that's where the Groovy Chicks, Pepper and Starshine, come in. These two wacky, Jesus-loving hippies are the original Groovy Chicks. Starshine and Pepper were born out of our desire to minister with humor and creativity, through our combined talents and passions.

Just What Is a Groovy Chick?

A Groovy Chick ...

1. Is groovy only because of Christ in her.
2. Yearns to share God's peace and approval with others and experience it herself.
3. Is still allowed to say (and mean) the words "cool" and "groovy."
4. Embraces the fact that God wants to use everyday people.
5. Loves people as Jesus does—with all their varied sizes, colors, and talents.
6. Adores having fun and celebrating life (even though this life is imperfect).
7. Appreciates old age, especially when it's staring her in the face.
8. Has, with God's help, found the best beauty secret of all: self-acceptance!
9. Isn't passive but is passionate about life!

10. Grows from trials and mistakes and ends up even groovier than she was before.

WE WANT TO SAY THIS LOUD AND CLEAR: WE MIGHT BE GROOVY CHICKS, BUT IT'S ONLY BECAUSE OF CHRIST'S LOVE IN US!

To be honest, we must admit that we don't "have it all together." We're not exactly what the world considers groovy. We're sure not fashionistas or fashion models, or even people who have all the answers. But we do know the One who is the answer! (Sing it with us: "Jesus is the answer, for the world today ...")

With Christ in our lives, we can be very groovy, indeed.

WHAT ARE ALL THOSE SIDE NOTES, ANYWAY?

You'll notice that along with every story, there will be a little something from Laurie (Pepper) or Dena (Starshine). We hope these sidebars will further encourage you on your road trip to love:

Pepper's Pit Stops are road trip guides for the weary or misguided. (Or they might just be really groovy ideas!)

Starshine's Smile Markers are quotes to inspire you and make you smile.

Pepper's Off-ramps are favorite offbeat road trip exits. Get ready for some really fun, unique exits.

Starshine's How's Your InnerState? are thought-provoking questions and journaling prompts. (Warning: Do not attempt to write while driving!)

Lost? Try GPS (God's Positioning System) are verses on love straight from the source—God's Word.

And who better to take you on the road than two crazy God-fearing hippies? So fasten your seatbelts, grab some snacks, and join Pepper, Starshine, and all our groovy friends on this road trip to love.

PART ONE

A LITTLE HELP FROM MY FRIENDS
(FRIENDS' LOVE)

THE MUTUAL ADMIRATION SOCIETY

ANNA JAMES

M y dearest friend, Lynn, looked in the mirror to check her face.

"I'm growing a mustache," she said.

"Really?" I hadn't noticed.

"Yeah, right here, see?" She leaned over and pointed to the top of her lip. The hairs there were light and blonde and barely noticeable, but yeah, she was growing a mustache.

I nodded sympathetically. "My friend swears by Surgi-cream."

She looked at me sideways and with a mischievous smile. "You might want to check yours, too."

I laughed but felt nervous enough to check. There they were, long brown hairs on either side of my lips, way worse than my friend's condition.

Yikes! How embarrassing to have to be *told* you're beginning to look like your old aunt. Still, I appreciated Lynn's honesty and her delicate approach.

True friendship is not for the faint of heart. Neither does it come quickly. A level of trust, respect, and mutual admiration needs to be in place before pointing out weaknesses or flaws. Had Lynn mentioned my "hair problem" the day we met or the first time we had tea together, the results would have been disastrous.

Over the years, Lynn and I formed a club called "The Mutual Admiration Society." Our bylaws state the following:

1. All members must frequently catch other members at their best—and then tell them so. "I am encouraged by how patient and calm you were with Billy when he put sand on your sandwich." Or "I am impressed by how you handled *insert difficult social issue here.*"
2. All members must notice and compliment the others on flattering haircuts. Addendum: All members must be sympathetic when said haircuts turn out to be unflattering.
3. All members must take each other's side when their boss (husband, sales clerk, mailman, etc.) is unpleasant.

It's possible for friendships to stay in the admiration phase where you hear nothing but "You're terrific," "You're funny," or "Those are the best butter cookies I've ever tasted!" Chances are, however, that these are the friends you rarely see—maybe only an hour on Sundays or at monthly PTA meetings.

When you spend real time with a friend, you begin to reveal your warts and flaws and, in return, you discover the failings and shortcomings of your friend. If your support for one another is genuine, the safety of your relationship and affirmation carries you through—and the richer aspects of The Mutual Admiration Society go into effect.

For example, my friendship with Lynn was put to the test when I moved across the country to the West Coast. New friends and adventures busied my days. At first I called her regularly to report that I had seen an orca whale, that I had lived through an earthquake, and that the rain really isn't so bad. But life got crazy, and as I settled in, my phone calls to my best friend lessened until they finally trickled down to almost nothing.

I went along my merry way for two and a half years with Lynn tucked fondly in the back of my mind. I thought everything was fine between us—until it was time for me to move back home.

Daydreaming about our glorious reunion, I called Lynn with the exciting news. She received my call joyously and celebrated right along with me. But as the conversation went on, I could tell something was bothering her. It wasn't easy for her to admit the truth. I could hear the hesitation in her voice, but eventually she spoke.

"It really hurt my feelings when you stopped calling and stopped returning my calls. I thought I didn't matter to you anymore." Ouch! I hadn't even realized what a terrible, selfish friend I'd been. I was quick to apologize and Lynn was just as quick to forgive me. When I returned home, it was as if I had never left.

Now I ask you, who but a real friend would call me on that? An acquaintance would not have pursued me wholeheartedly. A marginal friend would not have endured the awkwardness of voicing her hurt. She would not have done the hard work of truth telling to me. A lesser friend would have simply let me go.

The examples of Lynn's challenging love for me abound. As time goes by, the list—and our friendship—grows and grows. When I complain anxiously about some situation, my friend will ask firmly but kindly, "Have you prayed about it?"

When I'm really down, she listens closely and nods without giving any advice at all.

When I feel insecure, she reminds me that my worth, beauty, and identity are in Christ.

I always leave her house buoyant, carried in some way by her faith and pure heart. Her iron sharpens my iron and I am a better person for knowing her. I am stronger and more self-aware. I am loved—unconditionally, with no holds barred. I rest in the confidence that I cannot possibly be moody enough, proud enough, grumpy enough, or annoying enough for her to not love me.

The Mutual Admiration Society continues to meet every Friday over donuts and coffee. I tell my friend how much I like her new haircut and how much I admire her patience with the kids. I tell her how funny she is, and how smart. And I make sure to thank her for the times she carries me and remind her how much I love her.

And she says it all back.

Anna James lives in Philadelphia with her husband and two daughters. She is currently working on her first novel during her kids' naps and episodes of SpongeBob SquarePants.

GROOVY MOOVIES

PEPPER'S PIT STOPS

Groovy Moovies was so popular in our first book, *The Groovy Chicks' Road Trip™ to Peace*, we've decided to add another list. Groovy Moovies are clean, fun flicks to watch with fellow Groovy Chicks, including 'lil Chicklettes. These are the rare ones ... the movies that manage to be entertaining while keepin' it family friendly. Some even encourage deeper reflection, instead of jumping on the ever-popular "love 'em and leave 'em" bandwagon. So invite your girlfriends (including the younger ones), pop some corn, and enjoy!

Current faves:

- 😊 *Sense and Sensibility* (PG)
- 😊 *Cheaper by the Dozen* (PG)
- 😊 *A Cinderella Story* (PG)
- 😊 *Ice Princess* (PG)
- 😊 *The Incredibles* (PG)

And some older gems:

- 😊 *Sabrina* (1954 version)
- 😊 *The Sound of Music*
- 😊 *Roman Holiday*
- 😊 *The Harvey Girls*
- 😊 *The Philadelphia Story*

A Celebration of Life

PATRICIA LORENZ

Shortly before Valentine's Day, 2002, I received an e-mail from a good friend. I was already in the annual pre-Valentine's Day funk that causes single women like me who don't get Valentine candy, flowers, and fancy dinners to justify our disdain for the holiday. Many of us believe it's just an overly commercial fabrication created by card companies, flower shops, and candy manufacturers. We try desperately to ignore the hype while going about our daily business during the weeks before February 14—and wait for the day to be over.

But my perspective changed when an e-mail showed up on my screen. It was from Ray, my friend who still considers himself a newlywed, even though he and his bride tied the knot in August of 1999.

Two months earlier, Ray had been hospitalized for a bad case of pneumonia. Afterward, weak and homebound, he'd been kept under the watchful eye of his "bride," Geri.

Ray's letter talked about a daylong celebration he and Geri had on the day he finally felt well again. He wrote:

Our celebration yesterday began by thanking God for all his help ever since I had the scare exactly two months ago. After the antibiotics, taking it easy, and especially all the help and support from my beautiful resident physician (who wouldn't even let me take out the garbage for a couple weeks) I can say I'm nearly as good as ever. A great reason to celebrate.

And celebrate they did. Ray described their day in detail: They had breakfast together, walked around the mall (a feat, since he'd not had the energy to do that for quite a while), met friends for coffee, went to a movie, and came home to play cards. I felt thankful as I read that Ray had the strength for all those activities. But it didn't end there. A few days later he e-mailed again to describe his continued "celebration of life."

And the beat goes on! This evening we're taking in a St. Valentine's "Candlelight Evening for Couples" at our church, which will include liturgy, a presentation, sharing, and prayer, followed by a delicious, romantic, candlelight dinner.

We have so much to celebrate and thank God for, especially for his bringing Geri and me together. We're sure you have lots to be thankful for too. So, go ahead and celebrate. Be thankful every day of your life. And maybe just once in a while, enjoy a whole day of celebration. You don't need to look hard to find a reason. If you think about it, we all have many reasons to celebrate.

Something about my friend's words caused a change in me. That letter completely altered my attitude about holidays and celebrations. After reading it, I decided I would never again get wistful or jealous of my happily married friends during the Valentine season. The holiday may not visit me with a rainfall of heart-shaped baubles, fancy cards, or romantic dinners. But I sure can create my own celebration.

When I finished Ray's letter, I went out and bought my favorite treat—a box of crunchy milk chocolate Dove bars—and enjoyed one when I got home. Later, I called my kids who lived out of town and we all chatted like jaybirds. Then I prepared half a dozen cheery cards to send to a relative with terminal cancer. Finally, I finished a craft project to give to my oldest granddaughter for her birthday. I learned that the feeling of celebration is more about doing for others than desiring attention ourselves. All in all, it was a fabulous Valentine's Day, heartfelt to the core.

Another thing I learned from Geri and Ray is the fact that we certainly don't need a national holiday to plan a celebration. Pick a day, any day, and when you get out of bed that morning, declare it a grand day of celebration. You can celebrate freedom, family, good health, career, home, church, neighbors, friends ... everybody and everything.

On my next celebration, I may not pack as many things into a day as Ray and Geri did (who's got that much energy?), but it'll be wonderful just the same. Oh, did I mention that Ray turned 80 in 2004 ... and his bride is 72? Now *that's* worth celebrating!

Patricia Lorenz is a speaker and author of six books, including her latest, True Pilot Stories *(InfinityPublishing, 2005). She's also a contributing writer to over two dozen* Chicken Soup for the Soul *books (HCI). Visit www.PatriciaLorenz.com.*

STARSHINE'S SMILE MARKERS

Our love to God is measured by our
everyday fellowship with others and
the love it displays.

ANDREW MURRAY

MENTORING MELISSA

ELAINE YOUNG MCGUIRE

I didn't know Melissa when she began a mentoring program in our women's ministry, though we regularly attended the same service at our large church.

Older women were invited to participate, but when I heard, I thought, *Another program? I don't think this is for me, even though it is a great idea.*

The next week's announcement went something like, "There's only a little time left to sign up for our new mentoring program. We have a few spaces left for older women."

I was determined to avoid this new ministry, and I didn't budge. But I did feel a small urging from the Lord: *Maybe you could help a younger woman by talking about your own journey with me.*

I silently replied, *But, Lord, I thought we decided I would limit my involvement. You know how tired I am and that I just can't do everything that comes along anymore.*

When thoughts of joining the group occasionally bubbled to my consciousness again, I fought back, reassuring myself, *I've already been mentoring a young neighbor down the street. I don't think I need a "program" at church to put my faith into practice.*

Several weeks later, the church posted another notice which said, "Our new mentoring ministry for women is working well. We still have five young women left who desire to partner with an older woman, but so far, there have not been enough volunteers to fill this need. If you can help, please call the church office this week."

I should call, I thought, *and just do the best I can.*

Feeling a bit irritated, I wondered, *Now, where did that come from?* Deep down, I knew the answer.

Oh, all right, God, I prayed, without much enthusiasm. *If you're really telling me to join them, I'll call—but I still don't see how I can do this. You'll just have to help me!*

I made the call. And it wasn't long before I was told, "Melissa will be your partner. She's a young mother of two, in her thirties."

That's weird, I thought. *Melissa is also my daughter's name, and this Melissa is about the same age.*

I took down the information from the church office, then wrote Melissa a card and introduced myself. I pictured the young woman receiving it: a tired-looking young mother in baggy sweatpants, children tugging at each leg, all sitting among piles of unfolded laundry in her tiny starter home, with a dusty Bible lying on the coffee table.

That was easy enough, I thought, *but when will I find time to actually meet with her?*

When the next church bulletin announced a Christmas Cookie Swap for the mentors and mentorees, I still had not met Melissa. And the party was to be at her house!

I had trouble finding time to bake cookies, but eventually found an easy recipe. I rode to Melissa's house, thirty minutes away, with several other "older women." During the ride we teased each other, asking, "How did we get to be the 'older woman' so quickly? Where did all that time go?"

I was stunned when we drove into Melissa's upscale neighborhood. Her large, brick home was beautifully decorated, and she opened the door wearing a gracious smile to go along with her gorgeous outfit. "Thank you for coming," she said. "Elaine, I'm so excited to meet you."

Melissa had decorated her home with creative touches, including painted murals in the children's rooms. Pretty, handmade decorations were displayed around the house, in addition to several beautiful holiday trees.

Melissa introduced me to the group as her mentor and asked me to lead a prayer of welcome. She was the perfect hostess, smiling and moving among her guests, making us all feel right at home.

What could I possibly do for her, Lord? I wondered. She seemed to have it all together, and I doubted there was anything I could teach her.

Later she sought me out, and we had a little time to talk. It didn't take long to discover she was as pretty inside as outside. She had maturity and spiritual depth.

She explained, "When God put this idea on my heart, I went to Ruth, our Involvement Minister, to ask about starting it. We agreed to pray about it and, after we felt it truly was his will, we prayed over the pairing of each couple. Nothing was done according to our choice. We prayed over the two groups of names, written on small pieces of paper, and asked God to guide us in selecting the persons he wanted to work together."

Then she explained that since her own mother lived far away, she had longed for an older woman to help guide her spiritually. Even though it disappointed her to keep her own name out of the selection process, she knew there were never enough older women interested to balance the groups. She waited to see if the last four young women would be paired with late volunteers before indicating that she, too, wanted a mentor. Ruth had encouraged her, "Don't give up. God must have someone special reserved just for you."

"And then," she said joyfully, "you called!" I was humbled by her attitude and knew that to God, I must have sounded like Moses when he first made so many excuses about why he couldn't possibly lead his children out of Egyptian captivity.

I shared with Melissa how I had been brought practically kicking and screaming into the mentoring ministry. I felt ashamed that my stubborn will had nearly cost me the privilege of knowing this gracious young woman.

That was four years ago. Melissa and I never "fit the mold" in the mentoring program. We did get to know each other well, sharing several luncheon meetings and long talks on my screened porch while her children played in my yard. Later on we were able to attend a "Women of Faith" conference together. We have both been continually amazed at how alike we are and how similar our lives and spiritual struggles have been.

With my own grandchildren so far away it has been fun to sit together and to get Sunday morning hugs from her children and to give them special "I love you" gifts. They learned to eat green beans only after picking them from my little garden. Their sweet faces have places of honor on my refrigerator door.

In large and small ways, Melissa has blessed my life. When health issues forced my early retirement, she was one of the first friends on my doorstep, delivering a delicious meal, complete with a favorite cake she baked from a recipe I had shared with her.

A few months ago she was diagnosed with lupus, one of the same illnesses I've struggled with. Sometimes it is has been downright scary how much we have in common.

During one visit, she casually said, "I used to live in northern Virginia."

"Really? So did we!" I said. "Where did you live?"

"Arlington."

"So did we! When were you there?"

She told me, and I answered, "That's when we were there. You must have been just a baby."

"Yes," she said. "I was."

"Where did your family worship?" I asked, becoming more excited by the moment.

She answered and then added, "Daddy was the preacher there."

"I started a baby class at that church during those fourteen months we lived there!"

We stared at one another as the truth dawned, and I stated, "I must have been your first Bible study teacher!"

We were awed—and continue to be amazed—at the love of God, a love so great that he orchestrated these events in our lives and brought us together.

And as it turned out, I needed Melissa as much as she needed me.

Elaine Young McGuire, a retired teacher, writes from her home in Lilburn, Georgia. Her writing has appeared in many Christian publications, including The Upper Room.

Starshine's How's Your InnerState?

Mentoring

Questions for Reflection and Journaling

- ☺ Have you ever been in a mentoring relationship? If so, were you the mentor or the mentoree? If you haven't been involved in mentoring, would you like to in the future? Why or why not?

- ☺ Think of some of the mentoring relationships mentioned in the Bible (Naomi and Ruth, Paul and Timothy, etc.). What made them effective? How were the participants changed as a result of their friendship?

- ☺ Do you think mentoring is important? Why or why not?

- ☺ If you've learned and/or been changed by a mentor's guidance, take the time to write them a note of appreciation.

SELAH'S HOPE

JANE HAMPTON COOK

A male friend of mine took a pregnancy test just to prove to his wife that her test was positive," I said, trying to bring levity to the otherwise depressing meeting.

None of us wanted to be there, at Selah's Hope, but our private struggle with infertility had led each of us to the same point. We needed to talk with other women who shared our pain, who understood how a simple baby shower invitation or birth announcement could bring a torrent of tears and days of depression. We needed to be able to confess that sometimes we felt abandoned by God. We needed support, and friendship, and truth ... and hope.

So one frigid February night, we knocked timidly on the door of a Virginia house, one by one.

"Come on in," our hostess said as she ushered each of us into her cozy home for the first meeting of our church's newest ministry. The purpose of Selah's Hope was to provide infertile women with a community of hope, acceptance, encouragement, and understanding.

"The name 'Selah' comes from a term of rest used in the book of Psalms," one of our leaders explained.

After a devotional that first night, we went around the room and shared our most intimate problems with total strangers. Only a group of desperate, grieving women could be so vulnerable. One woman bawled as she told her story of recently learning from a doctor that she could not have children. Pursuing adoption was too painful for her to consider at that moment. She needed to grieve. After trying to conceive for three years, another woman had suffered an ectopic pregnancy, a dangerous condition and a painful loss.

The two group leaders were dealing with secondary infertility. Both had struggled to have their first child, and both hoped for a second one. They knew from experience how miraculous conception truly is and how elusive pregnancy can be. As each woman told her story, we cried through a box of tissues. Though strangers, we were on the same journey.

That night, I shared my three-year battle with infertility, which began when my husband and I moved to the Washington, D.C., area. Married seven years, we had recently served President George W. Bush in the governor's office in Texas. When my husband received an appointment at a federal agency, I joined the White House staff. Because of the intense stress, the average tenure of a White House staff member is only eighteen months, so I plunged into my new position with a plan to leave in a blaze of maternal glory within a year.

"What a great and graceful way to leave the White House," I said to my husband.

Having a child became my deepest desire, and as the months went by with no success, that desire became more important to me than my job at the White House. After a year of trying to conceive, we became eligible for tests covered by our insurance company. No major medical problems appeared. Another year passed. I quit work to relieve some stress. Still, nothing changed.

My friends who had children or who were pregnant couldn't relate to my struggle. They couldn't relate to my emotional pain or a new physical pain I was feeling on my left side.

The gals of Selah's Hope soon grew in number and closeness. We met every two weeks with the same formula: eating, praying, and updating the group on our situation. We motivated each other to keep moving forward by pursuing medical options or investigating adoption possibilities. We laughed and told stories. Sometimes we came to Selah's Hope with hearts weighed down by the anchor of our monthly grief. At other times we came with hope that next month would be "the month." We came up with a strategy. If you were down, you needed the group; if you were up, the group needed you.

Then it happened. The woman who had suffered through one ectopic pregnancy feared she was having another, but as it turned out, she was pregnant—and the baby had safely attached. Though we'd prayed for such a thing to happen, and we were quick to rejoice with her, we each sat quietly wishing we were the one needing maternity clothes.

Within a few weeks, one of the leaders called everyone.

"I'm expecting," she said.

Two prayers had been answered.

By spring, the pain on my side had grown to an almost daily occurrence—and along with it, my anxiety. Something was wrong. When tests failed to show a cause, my doctor recommended exploratory surgery, and we learned I needed laser treatment for endometriosis. The doctor touched me deeply when she took time to pray with me before the procedure.

"We don't know why endometriosis causes infertility, but it does," she said. "Because this disease can return within a few months, now is the best time for you and your husband to try to conceive."

I had renewed hope for a baby.

With summer approaching, the group agreed to hold one last Selah's Hope meeting before taking a break. Two seasons had come and gone since a group of strangers rang that bell for the first time. We were eager to see each other once more before the break, but I arrived at the meeting feeling hesitant. I wasn't sure how much I should share with my friends.

One by one we went around the table. When I counted and realized my turn would be last, I relaxed.

"All is well," the two "preggies" reported.

We rejoiced that their pregnancies were going smoothly. Another announced she'd be moving out of state, which was an answer to our prayers for her husband's unemployment. Another said that she and her husband had finally decided to pursue adoption.

Then it came time for the woman sitting next to me to speak. What she reported would determine what I would or wouldn't share. She had just gone through a third fertility treatment. Two earlier attempts had failed to result in a pregnancy. *Was she grief-stricken or filled with joy?* I wondered.

I held my breath. She had no idea how anxious I was to hear her update.

"I'm pregnant," she said.

She began to cry. Another baby, another prayer answered! Then it was my turn.

"I am pregnant, too," I said, unable to hold back my tears of relief and joy another moment. I had decided before the meeting that if my friends were down or grieving, I would not share my good news. I would wait for a more appropriate time to tell of God's miracle.

Of the seven of us there that last night, four were expecting. Like stair steps, our due dates spread over four consecutive months. But all of us, regardless of our pregnancy status, were in a better place as a result of the support and friendship of Selah's

Hope. God had performed miracles in each woman. With a little help from our friends, we had received God's promise to strengthen us and to give us a future—whether he answered our prayers for children or not.

We had hope.

Jane Hampton Cook is an author, speaker, and the former Deputy Director of Internet News Services for President George W. Bush. Originally from Texas, Jane currently lives in Alexandria, Virginia, with her husband and son.

STARSHINE'S HOW'S YOUR INNERSTATE?

Helping Those Who Grieve

Recently, some dear friends of ours had a stillborn infant. We longed to comfort them through their loss and show them Christ's love, but it's hard to know what to do to help other than to pray. What do you do when someone in your circle of friends suffers the death of a child, or a parent, or a friend? Do you fumble for words, or hesitate to call or write? Often, all a grieving person needs is a hug, an "I'm sorry," or a card that says, "I'm praying for you."

When my husband and I had a miscarriage early in our first pregnancy, people tried to offer comfort. Some of the things they did helped, and some didn't. Through that agonizing experience we learned valuable lessons about ministering to people in pain.

First, resist the impulse to fill silence. Sometimes people feel compelled to offer advice. When we lost our baby, one person said, "You're young. You can try again." Yes, I thought, but I wanted *this* baby. A well-meaning coworker of mine said, "It must have been God's will. Maybe your baby wasn't going to be healthy." While that may have been true, it didn't mean we didn't want him or her.

As a character in the recent movie, *Kingdom Come*, says: "Don't try to fix it; just let it be broken for a while." Sometimes a grieving person just needs a friend to sit with them. Sometimes all they need is a reassuring hug or a kind smile. If you're at a loss for words, say so. They'll understand.

Second, offer to do something practical. Does your friend need babysitting, a meal, or company on a shopping trip? Many people say, "Call me if you need anything," but few offer a specific service.

Third, send a card, flowers, or something else that would be meaningful to the grief-stricken person. Write the date of death on your calendar so you can send a card or flowers next year on the anniversary of their loss.

Finally, be sensitive to the Holy Spirit. If you feel a nudge to call a hurting friend at a particular time, don't ignore it. That may be God's way of letting you know they're struggling. A phone call or a card can mean the world to someone in the throes of despair.

I WANT TO KNOW YOU

LIZ COPELAND

Orders from the navy brought us together. I left our comfortable academic world nestled in the gentle mountains of Pennsylvania and came with my husband and our two small children. She came as a newlywed from the rolling hills of North Carolina.

Angie and I converged on a small island off the coast of Italy in the middle of the Mediterranean. I wore a reserved, scholarly, "spiritual" facade; she was a southern fireball.

I first noticed her at the navy chapel during a ladies' Bible study. She sat across from me at the far side of a long table crowded with women. As the study began, I watched Angie's presence fill the room.

She y'all-ed and drawled, and I sat mesmerized by her love of people. I envied her ability to make each woman feel as though she were the most important person in the room. I was drawn to Angie immediately. My lonely nature, which I had cultivated through years of hurt and self-protection, cried out for a friend.

After the meeting, I tentatively approached her. "I would like to get together sometime and discuss your views," my mouth stated matter-of-factly, but my heart was shouting, "I want to know you!"

"I'd like that soooo much," came her genuine reply. "Let's go to my place for some tea!"

We walked together through the narrow, winding cobblestone streets of the Italian island, our temporary home. Small, toothless women garbed in housedresses and bandanas waved from their courtyards. Words that sounded like gibberish flew from their smiling faces, but I did not understand. Angie didn't understand either, but she had her own way of communicating. "Buon giorno!" from her lips sounded a lot like, "Hey y'all!" The smile she returned to the signoras made her eyes completely disappear.

Old men stopped their game of checkers to nod their enjoyment of her presence. A policeman halted cars so we could pass to the other side of the street. The greetings he and Angie exchanged reminded me of an older brother teasing his little sister.

We made our way to a large apartment building that towered over its neighbors. Stucco peeled from the corners, and balconies protruded from each floor, showing off that day's laundry. Paned French doors and windows invited the sun to come and visit.

Before we reached the entry to her place, we heard a rush of syllables. It was Signor Fastami, Angie's landlord. He handed Angie a small wad of material. It seemed Angie's laundry had flown off the balcony ... again. Angie laughed at herself while holding up the silky panties. "Si, si, gracias!" she exclaimed, and they both chuckled at what I imagined to be a weekly ritual.

We continued our journey up the five flights of newly polished stairs. The wide marble steps narrowed as we reached our destination, and the angle of the door gave the impression that the apartment had once been an attic. Even before she opened the front door, warmth greeted me from the wreath that hung on the teak wood.

Stepping inside, I encountered ... her. Baskets of all shapes and sizes were tucked in corners, under tables, and on the walls. The smell of potpourri filled the room, and a bouquet of fresh flowers from the market found its place of honor on the simple wooden dining table. Crocheted pillows and lace memories graced the old (but quaint) furniture. And photographs in carefully chosen frames were displayed throughout the room. Her extended family lived with her ... even though they were across the sea.

My investigation turned toward the vibrant laughter coming from the balcony.

"I wish I knew how to keep my undies from escaping to Signor Fastami's!" Angie giggled as she picked up the remaining laundry from the sun-drenched tiles. I laughed with her while trying to think of a way to solve her problem. My chosen identity as "the fixer," the one with all the answers, began to surface. It was a way of having relationships that didn't get too close or messy.

"Let's have some iced tea," said Angie as she led me into her kitchen. "I swear I'm fixin' to turn into a puddle of soggy makeup before your eyes." As we drank, she wanted to know more about me. I gave her statistics.

I want out! something inside me cried.

But my nature countered, *Hush, you've nothing to say.*

Angie drawled and I sipped and her real self poured forth.

Beginning on that day, we met for tea and company regularly. Weeks passed, and then months. My walls began to crumble as I enjoyed her and she embraced me. I felt honored and thankful that Angie wanted to know me as much as I wanted to know her.

Together, we laughed, shared, cried, and tried—but failed— to master Italian. I learned I needed others and began to see people with new eyes of compassion, not as study cases. From Angie, I learned to love.

Eventually, we both moved back across the sea. Sometimes we have lived close, but mostly far away. Joy and sorrow, hilarity and pain have filled our lives, but I have not forgotten the lessons Angie taught me. I am now a true lover of people. I listen, enjoy, and give of myself in ways I never thought possible.

Every so often my friend and I opt to do more than just buy shares in our long-distance companies, and I go to see her. Entering her driveway, I see the flower-filled porch, a swing waiting for occupants, and an iron table set with iced tea.

And my heart says, *I'm glad I know you.*

Elizabeth Copeland currently resides in Van, Texas, with her husband, Jim, and three not-so-small children: Emilie, Seth, and Sarah. She teaches fourth grade at Van Intermediate School, hoping to instill a love of learning in her students.

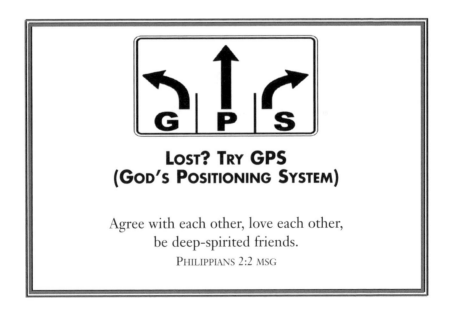

LOST? TRY GPS
(GOD'S POSITIONING SYSTEM)

Agree with each other, love each other,
be deep-spirited friends.
PHILIPPIANS 2:2 MSG

You're Not the Boss of Me

Peggy was a scary, mean, muscular girl with short hair who wore a constant scowl and licked a chapped ring around her mouth all day long. She'd push her way past me in line, knock my books off my desk, make ugly remarks about me on the playground, and sneer at the boys I liked. I got good grades and had other friends, but I wanted everybody to like me—including Peggy. She didn't. In fact, Peggy had despised me since kindergarten, and every year (to my great dismay) we ended up in the same class.

It was 1968, and we were in the fifth grade at George Washington Elementary School in Compton, California. What mattered were boys, go-go boots, the latest 45 single, and not being weird. In order to be liked, you had to be cool. You had to fit in. So you did everything you could do to be sure that happened: You wore the same styles as everyone else, used the same lingo, and held the same beliefs. To be singled out and treated differently was devastating, so Peggy's taunting—directed only at me—caused me great anguish.

One day, though, everything changed. To walk home from

school, I had to cross the small street in front of the campus. As Peggy's house was on the same side of the street as the school, she was not allowed to cross that street. The group I walked with had just cleared the crosswalk when I heard that dreaded voice.

"Hey Sharon," she yelled.

I almost didn't even turn around, but all the other kids— expecting some excitement—had stopped.

"What do you want now?" I sighed as I turned.

Peggy stood on the other sidewalk, flanked by Cindy, a big bruiser of a girl who followed Peggy around like a bodyguard. My heart began to beat a little faster. I felt like I was standing on a dusty road, with a saloon to my right and the sheriff's office to my left, staring down the enemy cowboy in the black hat. This was a definite showdown.

Then Peggy said the absolute stupidest thing I had ever heard. She squinted her eyes, placed her left hand on her hip, and pointed the index finger of her right hand as she commanded, "Come over here so I can kick your butt."

During the next few seconds, my brain processed her comment. *Why would I do that?* I thought. I would be walking right into an almost certainly painful confrontation. Surprisingly, my reaction wasn't one of fear, but of sheer disbelief at the ridiculous nature of that request.

Despite the eagerness of the crowd to see a fight, I simply said, "No." I turned my back on Peggy, made my way through the little group of kids, and walked home.

Peggy didn't like me and it didn't matter. She had singled me out big time and all the kids had expected me to act like they would have acted, but in that moment, I learned two things. First, I didn't need for everybody to like me. Some people would like me and some wouldn't. Peggy didn't; so what? Second, I discovered that neither taunting nor ugly words had the power to force me to do anything I didn't want to do. As the years went on, I found I could surrender that control to others if I chose to—and ultimately, I surrendered to God, who loves me and wants only the best for me.

Not caring what Peggy thought or said evidently took the wind out of her sails and she left me alone from then on. Peggy didn't know it, but she taught me to be an independent thinker that day. I never thought I'd say this but, "Thanks, Peggy! The day I refused to fight you was the day I became an individualist. And that has helped me every day of my life."

Sharon Norris Elliott's most recent book is What? Teenagers in the Bible? *(Pleasant Word Publishers). A popular event speaker, Sharon encourages her audiences toward a deeper relationship with God. She hails from southern California.*

Starshine's How's Your InnerState?

Imperfect Situations

Questions for Reflection and Journaling

☺ What imperfect situation is worrying you?

☺ How is God working in that situation? (If you don't know, take time to ask him to reveal the ways he is moving.)

☺ Can you think of ways you can "track" his faithfulness? (For example, by recording Scriptures that speak directly to your situation in a journal, or meeting weekly with a friend to recount God's blessings.)

FOIL FAIRIES

LAURIE BARKER COPELAND

Like Peter Pan, I simply refuse to grow up. Daily life might demand that I act my age, but when I go away for a weekend—to a women's retreat, for instance—look out! At forty-four, I still love to sneak around, toilet-papering cars and turning furniture upside down. My crowning achievement lies with aluminum foil. Yes—that's right. Silvery, shiny, skinny aluminum foil. Ah, the pure joy of using its moldable texture to create fanciful gifts. Though it's sometimes molded into swans at upper-class restaurants, foil is at its best when used as a quick pick-me-up.

Let me explain ...

Although I have been dubbed the "Master of Foil," I didn't *truly* master the art until I teamed up with Debbie, my dear friend and foil cohort. For years, I had challenged myself at our annual women's retreats to see how many rooms I could sneak into to decorate with the shiny substance. Careful to choose only those rooms whose owners would get a kick out of my escapades, I left my mark by transforming their footwear into elf shoes, complete with curled-tip toes. I even fashioned fabulous foil crowns. After several years, though, an absence of fresh ideas brought my sneak attacks to the brink of staleness. Until Debbie and I became roommates, that is.

Though she's melancholy by nature, Debbie has learned the value of a good laugh. So when we roomed together, I asked if she would be my "foil cohort." We were a perfect match! I showed her a new form of fun and made her laugh, and she took my art to new extremes.

Debbie shaped the thin metal into exquisite pieces of art: bracelets, necklaces, winged feet, Cleopatra circlets, even magnificent Minnie Mouse crowns. We performed our act on the sly, while a victim was out of her room. Before sneaking out of the room, we left our calling card—the words "Foiled Again" (sculpted, of course, from foil). We were a team, like George and Gracie, Ozzie and Harriet, Batman and Robin. We were ... the "Foil Fairies."

We negated our anonymity the following year when Debbie and I strapped wings of foil to our backs and began to blatantly crown unsuspecting women with our fantastic foil sculptures.

Are you thinking, *Silly! Preposterous!* or *What's the point?*

Wouldn't *you* love to be personally picked out, for no apparent reason, and crowned "Lover of Life," "Keeper of the Song Sheets," or "The Great Owner of Chocolate"? Our titles, regardless of how silly, brought smiles and happy feelings. People felt the joy of being loved and welcomed in the family of God. We were creating our own Fabulous Foil Sisterhood.

Grown, normally mature women came to us with their bottom lip stuck out, if they had not yet been "crowned." And we humbly obliged their requests. For an entire weekend, teenagers, mothers, and grandmothers alike proudly wore their crowns, elf shoes, and fun foil foolery.

What totally amazed me was how God used my silliness to bring joy to other women. He thought so much of me that he teamed me with an artist—a friend who would make being a Foil Fairy even more foil-y-er.

Rocky Balboa had something to say about this phenomenon. When referring to his wife, he held his hands out, fingers splayed to show the gaps, and said in his unforgettable voice, "Yo, Adrienne's got her gaps, and I got my gaps."

"But together," he said, folding his fingers into each other, "we ain't got no gaps." Pretty profound, right? As Christians, we know God can use anything and anyone. He can also take our gifts—from the profound to the silly—and fill in all the gaps to make us whole.

I am naturally silly and theatrical. Debbie is naturally serious and artistic. Together, we made a whole, and it resulted in grown women wafting around in creatively crafted crinkly crowns and elfin shoes.

Don't sell yourself short, and don't be "foiled." God created you specifically, with a purpose, instilling gifts in you that you may not yet recognize. Never be afraid to be who you are. He might have the perfect match to fill in your gaps and make you whole.

STARSHINE'S SMILE MARKERS

God often works in our lives, not by
giving us a perfect situation, but
by showing His power and love in
our very imperfect situations.
ALICE MATTHEWS
A WOMAN GOD CAN USE
(DISCOVERY HOUSE PUBLISHERS)

FIVE GROOVY WAYS TO SAY "I LOVE YOU" TO YOUR FRIENDS

PEPPER'S PIT STOPS

1. Clean her house when she's sick.

2. Invite her over for a fondue lunch or chocolate-dipped dessert (you'll find easy recipes online).

3. Offer to watch the kids for a day or weekend.

4. Take a personality test together and work on your communication.

5. Cut pictures of yourself into puzzle shapes and send in the mail to long-distance friends.

PART TWO

WE ARE FAMILY
(Family Love)

SERENDIPITY SISTER

ERIN KILBY

I hated Julie.

I hated her not because I really knew her, but because she was my brother Andy's *girlfriend*. I knew from experience that the girls who gravitated toward my brother were always the most popular, self-centered, and—oh, yes—the prettiest girls around.

Don't get me wrong—Andy was a fabulous brother. Three years older than me, he was an incredibly kind sibling, despite my slightly antisocial tendencies. As a freshman I was plump, quirky, dreadfully plain, and aware that Andy's radiant beauties were oblivious to my existence. I was jealous of their good fortune and resentful that they should not only be blessed with beauty, but with my brother's attentions—attentions that could have elevated my own status. So, one could say my hatred for Julie was born of habit.

By the time Andy started dating Julie, I was a confident senior, not part of the "in" crowd, but someone with a reputation as an artist and rebel who floated between playing softball and toting a flag in the band. My interests were unpredictable and noncommittal. I liked not fitting into a set mold. True to form, my boyfriend, Nate, didn't really fit in either. He had moved to our district shortly before the school year began, and I had added him to my list of varied interests. He was, of course, of the troublesome lot, a kid with a record and an alcoholic mother, but I had a soft spot for him. I felt that with a little work, I could mold Nate into someone "worthy" of my attentions in the few months left until graduation. Over time my noncommittal nature transformed, and I fancied we were in love, envisioning picket fences and minivans somewhere in our future.

Andy had recently moved back into our house to be closer to his local job. He commuted to classes at the university, and Julie called constantly. True to form, when I picked up the phone I was short, curt, and rude. "Andy, it's *that girl*," I would shout through the house and drop the phone noisily on the counter. He'd frown at me and pick up the phone.

To my chagrin, Julie was undaunted by my hostility. She always spoke to me politely on the phone and warmly when she visited the house. *What is with her?* I wondered. *Does she not understand a cold shoulder?* I kept ignoring her.

I was a senior, very clever—at least in my own mind—and wise to her schmoozing. She was cute like Andy's previous girls, and I was not about to invite her into my life, only to see her morph into some pretentious prom queen.

And then one Saturday, while my parents were out of town, it happened. Nate's mother called me because she discovered a note in her son's pants from Jennifer, one of my closest friends. This friend, whom I had trusted implicitly, had gotten pregnant, and Nate was the father. In one short phone call, the future I'd painted on canvas began to streak, melting all the pretty images and blending all the brightness into bleakness.

Up in my room, I cried until I thought I would surely die from dehydration. Evening came; I was alone and absolutely miserable. But, the last thing I wanted to see was my brother's car—and Julie's blonde hair through the window—as they drove up the driveway.

The laughing couple tumbled through the door, arms filled with packages and cheeks flushed from enjoying one another's company. Their obvious pleasure made my chest feel like it rested beneath cinder blocks. That's when Julie caught my eye. "What's wrong, Erin?" she asked and dropped all her packages. She sat down beside me on the edge of the chair and leaned forward, tilting her head so that she could look into my swollen eyes.

I glanced up at Andy. "Nothing," I said stoically.

Her eyes left mine only briefly, just long enough to dart up at Andy. I can only guess the message that was written there. *Go, Andy,* they must have said. *She needs me, and I can handle this.*

We ate pizza that night at a local restaurant. (It could have been raw snails; I wouldn't have noticed.) The only thing I remember is that I became the center of Julie's world. She listened to me boy-bash—something I desperately needed. She sympathized with womanly grace, and not once did she condescend to me like the older, wiser lady that she was. She transformed into the sister I never had, and I basked in her warmth and affection.

Years later I stood in the church as Julie's bridal attendant and witnessed her "I do's." That day, Julie became my sister-in-law, but she was already my sister in spirit. Since that night long ago when I entered the adult world, Julie has stood by my side with unfailing love. She held my hand when my father passed away. She shared the angst of fertility visits and failed pregnancy tests. She gave me a sweet baby nephew named Cale who reaches up to me with his mother's warm affection. And even though I live halfway across the country now, too far away to have regular visits, Julie remains close and connects with me regularly through letters and phone calls, just like always. She is patience, grace, and forgiveness.

And I love her.

Erin Kilby resides in Kingwood, Texas, with her family—Michael, Tyler, and Chelsea. She has published works in anthologies and magazines and is currently writing her first novel. You may reach her at erinkilby@hotmail.com.

STARSHINE'S SMILE MARKERS

Love can't be pinned down by a definition, and it can't be proved, any more than anything else important in life can be proved. Love is people, is a person. A friend of ours, Hugh Bishop of Mirfield, says in one of his books: "Love is not an emotion. It's a policy." Those words have often helped me when all my feelings were unlovely. In a summer household as large as ours I often have to act on those words. I am slowly coming to understand with my heart as well as my head that love is not a feeling. It is a person.

MADELEINE L'ENGLE

A Circle of Quiet

(HarperSanFrancisco)

What a Difference a Day Makes

B R E N N A   R H O D E S

Wednesday morning started as usual: kids and babies crying for breakfast, husband rushing off to work in a blur, me lamenting the fact that I don't even get time for a cup of hot tea, much less toast. I jammed my hair into a ponytail with one hand while I stirred the eggs and poured the juice with the other. I am the queen of multitasking—never mind that I may not even get the chance to change out of my robe before the day ends.

By lunchtime, I was permanently stooped from picking up puzzles, Legos, blocks, cars, books, stickers, crayons, bears, dolls, cups, blankies, binkies, trains, shoes, and Cheerios. I spent thirty minutes getting one toddler to sleep for his nap, only to have him wake up just as I was laying the other toddler in his crib. Drat! No naptime meant I would just have to postpone my trip to the bathroom. *No problem,* I figured. *I can hold it. AGAIN.*

We spent the afternoon outside. My daughter wanted me to push her in the swing, and while I was distracted, one son made a snow angel (we live in Texas, so he just used mud) while the other ate a June bug. All three kids were so dirty I had to strip everyone down to their skivvies when we were ready to come back inside. My husband arrived home and we exchanged a quick peck and partial sentences about our days while the little ones fought for our attention.

The evening passed in a blur of a meal fixing, feeding, teeth brushing, and dressing everyone for bed. After tucking in and praying with the last kid, I faced a sink full of dishes, a porch piled with muddy clothes, and the living room floor strewn about with toys like stars across the Milky Way.

What's the point? I thought. *I am unappreciated, overextended, and exhausted. If only I could get some help, some understanding, some praise for all I do for everyone around here*, I grumbled while grudgingly finishing up the day's chores. I fell into bed mumbling a prayer filled with no thanksgiving—just requests for more energy and appreciation from my family.

The next day—a day I'll always remember—God changed me completely. I learned about another mother, Carol, who was in the hospital on a respirator, her thirty-eight-year-old body ravaged by lymphoma. I had known Carol was sick for several weeks, but that Thursday I received detailed information about her poor prognosis, her desperately hopeful husband, and their ten precious and confused children. Caught off-guard, I wept as I thought of this family's suffering.

My mind raced. I ached, thinking of all the things Carol must have longed to do but couldn't. What did she miss the most? What would she give all her earthly possessions to have once again? I didn't need to ask Carol; I knew the answer to those questions because I am a mother too.

I was certain that in her dreams she was home again, snuggling babies, kissing boo-boos, preparing family meals, and teaching her children. I knew she would love to tenderly wipe a nose, praise a potty-training toddler, or hold a frightened child in the night to soothe away a nightmare. But Carol couldn't feel or experience any of those everyday things. I took a meal to the family that night, and prayed for Carol and her family when I went to bed. Then I wept some more and prayed for my ungrateful self.

Friday morning began the same as always, but *I* was not the same. The new me stood at the stove scrambling eggs in the same messy kitchen with the same scurrying husband and the same whining toddlers, but it looked completely different to me now. God had given me the vision to see my life, my existence on this earth, with clarity.

First Thessalonians 5:18 ran through my head all day: "In everything give thanks; for this is the will of God in Christ Jesus for you" (NKJV). God didn't say in every great thing, or in every wonderful thing. He didn't say to be thankful for a spa day or give thanks when we inherit a fortune. He said give thanks in everything. I am sure that is just what he meant, too.

So I thanked him for all of it on that Thursday—and I've continued to thank him for my blessings: for being able to stand upright in this kitchen on a crisp morning; for my loving husband, his job, his commitment to our family, and his willingness to pitch in, even if he can't fold a fitted sheet or find the ketchup in the refrigerator. I thank God for my healthy kids—for their beautiful smiles, dimples, and giggles. For how delicious they smell after a bath. For the blessing that those sticky cheeks are mine to kiss and those sweaty hugs are for me! I am thankful they can run, even if they drip Popsicle juice as they go. I am grateful they can sing, even if they do it very loudly while I am on the phone. The new me wakes up every morning now and thanks God for the moment when he kicked the old me out. Now, I begin each busy day with a prayer. I thank him for every happy, silly, joyful, challenging, difficult moment I will face in the coming hours. I don't let everyday slices of life (even warts!) slip by me anymore without being thankful to just be a part of it all.

I like this new me—the one who smiles more. The one who spends less time fretting and more time enjoying life. The one who speaks prayers of thanksgiving and praise for small (and large) blessings from above.

Most importantly, the new me is more in tune with our heavenly Father. You know what? On those days when the old me used to complain to God that I felt unappreciated by those who love me, I bet God was saying, "I know just how you feel."

Brenna Rhodes lives in Texas with her husband and their three young children. She enjoys homeschooling, spending time with her family, gardening, cooking, and reading. She also loves writing about God's blessings in her own life.

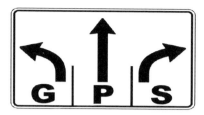

Lost? Try GPS
(God's Positioning System)

On your feet now—applaud GOD!
Bring a gift of laughter,
sing yourselves into his presence.

Know this: GOD is God, and God, GOD.
He made us; we didn't make him.
We're his people, his well-tended sheep.

Enter with the password: "Thank you!"
Make yourselves at home, talking praise.
Thank him. Worship him.

For GOD is sheer beauty,
all-generous in love,
loyal always and ever.
PSALM 100 MSG

LETTING GO

CINDY O'HALLORAN

I walked toward the entrance and hesitated. The door creaked just a bit as I opened it.

"Hi Mike," I said, walking in. My, he looked handsome in his tuxedo. "I thought I would come and offer some last words of wisdom."

Mike looked at me from under his eyebrows with that familiar smirk. He stood, quietly waiting for me to say something. I'd come in to give a wise word, something worth remembering, but I couldn't think of anything to say. I had already taught him all I knew, regularly offering my opinions—and now the most important day of his life had arrived and I was speechless.

A tear rolled down my cheek and he opened his arms to hold me, his last hug as a single man. I tilted my head back to stop the tears and took a deep breath. He loosened his hug and glanced at me.

"What are you doing?" he asked.

I cleared my throat to hide my embarrassment. "I was once told that if you feel yourself starting to cry, just tip your head back, take a deep breath, and you'll gain control again."

Mike tipped his head back and took a deep breath. "Those were excellent words of wisdom, Mom. Thanks."

"Are you ready?" I asked, squeezing him one more time.

"Yes, Mom. Let's go."

The music started to play. Mike escorted me to my seat and then took his place at the front of the church to await his bride.

The church glistened with decorations, but my eyes focused on the unity candle. Two tapered candles surrounded it, their flames flickering and dancing. I had lit the right one, the one symbolizing Mike as an individual. Soon it would join with his bride's candle, and together, both they and the flames would become one.

I watched Mike's face as his bride came into view. He stood in awe, his eyes fixed on her glowing smile. As she stopped next to him and he took her hand, thoughts of time spent with my boy raced through my mind. I stared at him, remembering a six-year-old digging in the yard.

"Mom, I found dinosaur bones!" he yelled, running in the back door, dirt blowing from his hands as he unveiled the skull.

"Mike!" I shrieked. "That's not a dinosaur. It's the rabbit we buried last year!"

I smiled at that thought, barely holding back a snicker. He thought he had found a real treasure that day!

As I sat there listening to the pastor, my mind wandered. I pictured Mike in his black snow pants and Packers' jacket at the age of thirteen. He stood at the outside door with his fingers wrapped tightly around his sled, pleading with me to go sledding. So I bundled up, and together we hiked the big hill at the back of our property. We trudged through mounds of snow, grabbing onto tree branches for support. I paused to catch my breath, but Mike was determined to conquer that hill. His wind-burned cheeks sparkled as he smiled. Two hours later, we made it to the top.

With anticipation, Mike positioned the sled and sat on it. I nestled in, wrapped my arms around him, and grabbed onto the rope. But as the weight of the two of us pushed the sled down and we sank into the snow, I laughed. Mike's teeth clenched in frustration. Determined to make it work, he stood up and trampled down the snow in front of the sled, smoothing it out to give us a slippery start.

He then took his position again and away we went, dodging trees and flying over snow drifts. What took two hours to prepare for ended in a ten-minute, unforgettable, glorious ride.

I stopped daydreaming when the pastor announced it was time to light the unity candle. As Mike turned to face his bride, a tear dripped from my cheek to my lap. *Would things still be the same?* I wondered.

Watching my son look at his bride as the two of them brought their flames together, the reality finally hit me. My boy, now a man, was getting married today. Things would never be the same. The Lord tore the bond we had woven over the years and it was time to let go.

Mike's determination to wait on the Lord paid off: He had found a treasure in Lyndsay. Her charm and pure heart had swept him off his feet. Now, she stood next to him and together they lit the central pillar. At the moment his breath extinguished the tapered candle I had lit, the last of the tearing took place. The string that connected my heart to his snapped and joined itself to Lyndsay's heart. But my heart, expecting sadness, soon filled with joy. I knew that even though life with my son would never be the same, the Lord had a plan. The look in his eyes as he gazed upon his bride filled me with that assurance.

Before I knew it, the pastor pronounced them husband and wife. This was the happiest-saddest day of my life. As I walked toward the reception line to give my new daughter a hug, she smiled at me. "I will take good care of him. I promise," she whispered.

I smiled and we embraced. "Lyndsay," I said, "I knew the day would come when I would have to let Mike go. I couldn't be more pleased knowing God chose *you* to love him."

I will always be Mike's mom, but I no longer hold the responsibility of caring for him. He now cleaves to his wife. Loving my son meant letting him go.

Cindy O'Halloran of Richland Center, Wisconsin, is a book reviewer for the syndicated column What's Up? *which appears in several Christian newspapers in North America. She is a published short fiction writer and teaches fiction writers through her Web site, www.writershelper.com.*

STARSHINE'S SMILE MARKERS

The reality of our communion with Christ and in him with one another is the increase of love in our hearts.
WILLIAM TEMPLE

JOURNEY TO AMELIA

CHRISTY LARGENT

We were the last ones up in the elevator. I, the one who always liked to be first, dragged my feet. Magnanimously, I had insisted everyone else in our group go on ahead of us. Finally, my husband Tom, my mother, and I, along with two strange little men carrying bulky boxes, were squeezed into the tiny elevator and hauled, herky-jerky, up to the fifth floor. On that floor my life would change forever, and for some reason I felt like stalling.

You see, I had waited for this moment for almost forty years. The fifth floor held the culmination of a dream that went back as far back as I could remember. The dream incubated while I "nursed" my baby dolls as a toddler. It was nurtured and strengthened in my heart through years of babysitting, bossing, and believing I would someday be a mother.

Through life's usual twists and turns (or perhaps, God's unusual sense of timing), the dream had died many times. I felt rather panicked at it finally coming true today, this afternoon, in a city ten thousand miles from home, in a land where I couldn't understand the simplest comment, in a country so ancient and full of mystery. It felt as if it were all a mirage. I feared that when those elevator doors finally opened, it would all just disappear in an instant.

But when those doors opened, the mirage became reality. Noise and confusion and screaming babies and laughing parents and flashing cameras confirmed it. The dream was coming true! And of course, as reality so often is, it was nothing like what I had envisioned. The adoption caseworkers had told us to expect an orderly handoff, like a school graduation. The babies were supposed to be waiting quietly with their caregivers. The parents would then be called up to the stage one by one, and the caregivers would proceed up to the stage, making the handoff. We would take a group picture, and everyone would move forward, happily enjoying their new lives together with their new babies.

But that wasn't what was happening. Instead, bedlam ensued. Everyone I had allowed to go ahead of us already had their babies, the facilitators dashed about, and where was my Amelia? What was going on?

All of a sudden I thought I saw her. Our little "Fu Ai Yan," soon to be Amelia Ai Yan, sat stone-quiet, expressionless yet alert, in the lap of an old lady. She stared at me, rather like the stare of a baby raccoon I spotted one night from my kitchen window. My Amelia was wary, tense, anxious, and a little bit defiant. In spite of the uncertainty, she let me know who was in control.

I could tell I had to tread lightly, so I stopped about ten feet away. I looked at her, and she looked at me. Nothing, no movement, just the intense stare. I gazed back and leaned slightly forward, afraid to approach. Voice trembling, nauseated with the intensity of the moment I said, "Hi baby." She stared at me.

"Hi honey," I crooned encouragingly. She stared, mute. "Amelia? It's me, Mama," I said, pointing at myself.

Another look, a startled little yelp of terror, then silence again. "Go pick her up," my mother urged. But I was afraid to move.

My thoughts whirled. *Go pick her up? Was I really sure this was Amelia? Should I pick her up? Could I pick her up? What was going on?*

"Go on, Christy," my mother insisted. "Go get her and I'll start videotaping." Tom, silent himself, stood calm and steady at my left elbow. I crept towards Amelia and tentatively reached out my arms. Then, finally, my daughter was in my arms.

I looked her over carefully as I nuzzled her neck and snuggled her sturdy little body. Her round cheeks were like incandescent cherries, her dark silky hair was plastered to her head, and her exquisite almond eyes were piercing—so dark and deep you couldn't see the pupils. She'd been bundled into three layers of clothes and topped with an Easter-egg-blue snowsuit. She looked like a fat, perfect, little one-year-old China doll.

My China doll. She intensely studied me for about three minutes. Then, as if her decision had been made, she averted her head as far from me as she could get, arched her little back, and began to shriek.

So much for the fantasy! She screamed. She sobbed. Actually, she screamed and sobbed for the next seven hours. She wanted nothing to do with me, and would only calm a bit when Tom held her. Every time I looked at her, in fact, she screamed anew.

She didn't stop bawling until she fell, exhausted, into a deep sleep that evening. She squealed when she woke up about midnight, and would not be comforted until Tom took her into bed with him, displacing me into the other bed. She screamed as I tried to cuddle her close the next morning. While Tom showered and I tried to nurture my precious daughter, she just sobbed "Ma-ma, Ma-ma," over and over as if her heart were splitting apart. When Tom got out of the shower, *two* sobbing females greeted him.

How could this be? Motherhood wasn't supposed to be like this. Amelia was supposed to love and adore me! Instead, she rejected me. Intellectually, I knew she would come around. *Girls always bond with their mothers, right?* I reasoned. *This is just temporary as she mourns the loss of her foster mother.*

I tried to convince myself that I just needed to allow her a time of grieving so she'd be free to love and bond with me later, but inside I felt catatonic. Only I couldn't show it on the outside. How selfish of me that would be!

My heart began to harden. I had risked reaching out for this miracle called "motherhood," and had been slapped for my efforts. Once again, as the disappointment triggered every relational failure in my life—I mean, even Duffy Finnerty rejected me when I asked him to the Sadie Hawkins dance in ninth grade—my mind raced through the litany of why I didn't deserve love anyway.

What did I expect? Of course she would reject me. What made me think I deserved to be a mother anyway? Why should she love fat, lazy me? And … and … "It's all about you Christy," the father of lies softly murmured in my ear. "It's all about you."

The cock crowed and I wept. Well, actually Amelia screamed, but the effect was the same. I suddenly remembered who the father of lies was. It certainly wasn't my heavenly Father, who had prepared this wondrous event in advance for me from the beginning of time. It was the enemy. And as the enemy always does, he did his best by attacking my soft spots so he could steal my joy.

And I had believed him.

Thankfully, the Holy Spirit (via the ear-piercing howls of Amelia) suddenly reminded me that it was about *so much more* than me. It was all about unconditional love, and the fact that the love I first received from Christ is the love I had to give my Amelia—no matter how many times she averted her face, arched her back, and screamed bloody murder. It was about loving because he first loved us. It was about giving myself to something much bigger than my plans and desires.

And suddenly I knew it would all be okay. We would make it through this. We would trust God for his perfect plan. He knit this family together in his own unique and miraculous way, and we would trust him to see us through.

And while we waited, we'd invest in a really good pair of earplugs.

Christy Largent is a speaker and author who is passionate about empowering people to revolutionize their relationships by strengthening their people skills. Christy lives in Redding, California, with her husband Tom and their daughter Amelia. Visit her Web site, www.christylargent.com.

STARSHINE'S SMILE MARKERS

It is not a matter of thinking a great deal but of loving a great deal, so do whatever arouses you most to love.
MOTHER TERESA

No More Grumbling

MARLENE BAGNULL

From the day my husband picked it out and brought it home, I grumbled about "that car." It didn't matter that it got almost triple the gas mileage of my station wagon or that it had been a good buy. Nothing Rob* said could win me over.

About the same time, our eighteen-year-old daughter experienced "love at first sight."

"Don't you think you're too young to get serious so quickly?" we cautioned.

"I'm the same age you were when you married Dad," she replied. "And haven't you and Dad said you immediately knew you were meant for each other?"

What could we say? It was true. Rob and I had fallen in love on our first date. He was twenty and I was seventeen, and eighteen months later we married. Our parents thought us too young, but twenty years of marriage had proven our love was the real thing. But Donna and Harold's relationship? I wasn't so sure. I became even more uncertain as summer wore on.

*Names have been changed

77

Something made me uncomfortable. Perhaps it was Harold's background. I didn't know much more about him than I did about that car. And what I did know made me uneasy.

When Harold was twelve, he ran away from home because his father drank and beat him. After that, he ran away from every foster home he lived in until, finally, at sixteen, he found someone he trusted. Nine years later he was still living with his foster dad. I wondered if he could make it on his own.

I talked to a friend who knows my daughter almost as well as I do. I knew she would tell me if I was overreacting or being prejudiced. She shared my discomfort.

"Harold may be a wonderful young man," she said, "but I can't help feeling he's another one of Donna's causes."

I cringed, remembering the last boy Donna dated. He had spent several years in a juvenile detention center. Donna was determined to help him solve his problems. Eventually, he got his life together, but then he walked out of hers.

Donna's father had other concerns. "How is Harold going to support you?" he asked. "He barely earns more than minimum wage. He doesn't have a car or his own apartment."

"We'll make it," Donna said. "You and Mom did."

Again we had no comeback.

"But what about your college education?" he persisted.

"I'll keep going," she promised.

"How?"

"Come on, Dad. The community college isn't *that* expensive, and my nursing course is only two years long."

"Yes, two long years of study and hard work," I added. "How will you juggle that *and* marriage?"

Several months later Donna dropped out of college. I felt furious when I found out.

"It's my life!" she said.

"But how could you let us believe you were still going to classes?"

She shrugged.

"It's Harold, isn't it?" I said. "You've changed so much since you've met him. I don't understand you anymore."

"You don't want to understand," she snapped. "You've *never* liked Harold. You've wanted to break us up since we met!"

"That not true, Donna. Dad and I are just concerned about you."

"Well, you don't need to be concerned."

That evening, Rob had no words to console me. We both knew we were losing our daughter. It didn't help to know that we parents raise our children so they can leave us. Everything in me screamed that this was not the way or the time or the right man for my daughter.

I began looking for every opportunity to show Donna the mistake she was making. I grumbled about the way Harold treated her. "Love is blind, but you'll see what I'm talking about once you're married to him."

"No, you'll see how blind you are, Mother," Donna said sarcastically.

Something in me snapped, and I began to cry. Donna stared at me, her face like stone. "Oh Donna," I sobbed, "if you marry him we won't ever see you."

"That's not true, Mom," she said, softening a little. "You'll see even more of us."

Her words didn't quell my fears.

We hoped they would wait at least a year—or at least until they could afford an apartment of their own. But a week before Christmas, Donna and Harold informed us that they were getting married New Year's Eve—by a justice of the peace. "We'd like you to come," she said, "but whether or not you do, we're getting married."

Nothing we said could dissuade them. When Donna walked out the door that evening, we knew she was walking out of our lives.

We went to the wedding as spectators, not participants. Donna hadn't asked her dad to give her away. She didn't wear the gown she and I had purchased that summer. If there was a reception, we weren't invited. Rob and I came home to a house that felt empty, despite the presence of our two younger children.

Almost as if my words had been prophetic, Donna dropped out of our lives. For the next twelve days, we didn't even know where she was living. It felt like twelve weeks! Then she made a visit (two days late) for my birthday. After that, we saw her only sporadically.

However, I was determined not to be an interfering in-law. Donna and Harold were married—from my perspective, for life. I made it a point not to say anything negative about Harold. I didn't say anything positive about him either, but at least I didn't grumble about him to Donna, as I did to my husband and to anyone else who would listen.

Fifteen months after Donna's marriage, without warning or legitimate reason, my husband lost the job he'd held for nine years.

"Maybe this is a sign that God intends to move us," Rob said, trying to be optimistic.

He had been looking for a position down south for six months, but nothing had opened up. Now, he suddenly started receiving calls about available jobs.

Rob and I headed south in the car I still disliked as intensely as I disliked my son-in-law. Of course it gave us one problem after another. It was a miracle it got us to the retreat center where we had planned to spend a few days. While Rob went on interviews, I nursed my anger and bitterness over the job loss, Donna's marriage, and that car.

On the morning we were getting ready to leave the retreat

center, a new friend pulled me aside. "There's something I want you to do first," she said.

"What?" I asked, puzzled by the urgency in her voice.

"See that car out there?"

"Yes," I replied as I glared at it. After the problems it had caused us on this trip, my negative feelings about it were stronger than ever.

"You know that car would run much better if you gave it a bath."

"A what?!"

"You heard me. All you've done since you've gotten here is grumble about that car. You need to treat it with more kindness and respect."

"Respect?" The word caught in my throat. She had to be joking, but she wasn't. She got a bucket, and together, we gave it a good scrubbing.

"No more grumbling," she reminded me as we said good-bye.

Two days later, on the final leg of our trip, I opened my Bible. What I read there stunned me: "Don't grumble about each other, brothers. Are you yourselves above criticism?" (James 5:9 TLB).

Like a videotape on playback, the events of the past fifteen months flashed before me. Suddenly, I saw areas where I had been wrong.

"God, forgive me for the way I've treated my son-in-law," I prayed silently.

The Lord's response was clear. He wanted me to ask Harold for forgiveness.

"But Lord," I protested.

I sensed his answer. It didn't matter who was right or wrong. Harold was now part of my family. I needed to love and accept him.

The car I had grumbled so much about became the Holy of Holies, as God's love and forgiveness filled me.

As soon as we got home, I went to see Donna and Harold.

"Harold, will you forgive me—for everything?" I asked.

His hug said it all.

Our relationship is not totally healed, but the wall between us is crumbling. Some days I'm still tempted to say something negative about him, but God reminds me of my friend's words, "No more grumbling," and he draws my attention to *that* car. It has not given us a single problem since I started treating it with respect and kindness.

I guess that's all any of us really needs.

Marlene Bagnull is the author of five books and compiler/editor of three others. The author and her husband have three grown children and one grandchild, with another on the way.

LOVE ISN'T FOR WIMPS

Wilma's personality wasn't appealing and she made poor clothing choices, but more than that, she had an unattractive attitude. She didn't have a *bad* attitude—she just irritated the other students by loitering in the hallway, asking insignificant questions, or by waving her arm in class after every question, though seldom knowing the right answer. She also smelled.

My dad, a high school teacher, genuinely disliked her.

Dad knew he was living in contradiction to God's will and that he should love Wilma. It embarrassed him that he couldn't. It just seemed impossible.

But he decided to try. So every day before entering the classroom he prayed, "God, help me love Wilma." Impossible. But he persisted with, "God, help me love Wilma."

As the days passed, he noticed his attitude beginning to change. And one day, he called Wilma to his office. As my dad looked at her face, he realized he no longer disliked her. At that point, he simply pitied her. He asked if she knew why the students disliked her, and she said she didn't.

He said, "Would you like me to tell you some things that may help you?" She nodded a yes. As tenderly as possible, my compassionate dad shared with her his observations and suggestions. Then he finished by asking, "Wilma, do you think I would make these suggestions if I didn't like you?"

She thought awhile and then answered, "No. I think you like me."

He took a deep breath and decided to broach the next subject. "Wilma, I would never tell you the next suggestion unless I loved you …" With another quick breath, he said, "Wilma, take a bath."

Guess what? She took the advice to heart and cleaned up! She also completed Dad's class, and every so often, she flagged him down eagerly in the hallway to tell him how things were improving.

But the true surprise for my dad was what happened in his own heart. He had beseeched God to change his resentment to a genuine love … and God answered that prayer.

Sometimes it's tough to tell (or hear) the truth. But who ever said love was for wimps?

ALWAYS CARRY A HANKY

DENA DYER

During a friend's funeral, the pastor related several of the answers he received when he asked my friend's grandchildren, "What kind of things did your pop teach you?"

Some were typical answers, such as "Pay back your debts" and "Work hard and you'll be rewarded." One response was funny: "Righty tighty, lefty loosey" (for opening jars and lids). But then came my favorite answer: "Levers are our friends."

I laughed out loud to my husband's chagrin, since no one else found it funny. I'll acknowledge that laughter is not always the recommended response at a memorial service. But it struck me as quirky, random—and hilarious.

Later, I got to thinking about the things my own family members taught me. I've written about my grandma, hubby, and kids a lot, since their lessons loom large in my life. And I've written about my mom (one of my best friends) pretty often too. But it only seemed appropriate in a book on love to write about the other person who has loved me as hard and long as Mom has: my dad.

Some of the lessons Dad has taught me were observed and

others were drilled into me. All of them have practical applications. For instance:

Get an education. I would have gone to college anyway, but summers spent on our family ranch hoeing up weeds, planting trees, and cleaning out stock trailers made the option much more attractive. In his youth, Dad spent long hours picking cotton, and that back-breaking work was his impetus to succeed. He ended up as a lawyer and county attorney, and he ranches for "fun." (I'll let him do the ranching—give me air-conditioning and the comfort of my reading chair any day!)

I'm here for you. My mom and I have a very close relationship, a reality my dad appreciates and enjoys. He knows that moms and daughters have a unique bond, and he isn't jealous of the time we spend together or our talks on the phone. The thing is, Dad has made it clear by his constant support and presence in my life that he "has my back." I know that wherever I go and whatever I do, he's there if I need him ... and he loves me.

Kids are worth your sacrifice. Dad loved leading music part-time at our little church in Dumas, Texas. He adored singing, preparing music for the choir, rehearsing with them, and leading the congregation in hymns. My mom played the piano, and they often sang duets. We spent a lot of our free time at the church, and Dad often says I was "weaned on a hymnbook."

However, he gave up his position at Calvary Baptist when my brother and I grew old enough to be in a youth group. Calvary didn't really have one, and the other Baptist church in town (which was quite a bit larger) had a wonderful youth choir program, complete with cross-country mission trips each summer. After much prayer and discussion, Daddy agreed to step down and give us the opportunity to participate in those activities. That sacrificial act spoke volumes about what it means to "lay down your life" for someone else (a lesson I refer to sometimes with my own kiddos).

Keep your money, your car, and your body in shape. When Dad called me after I moved away to attend college, our conversations centered around my bank account (which often dwindled), my health (he wanted to know if I was exercising or if I was staying up too late), and my car. Even though it irritated me that he seemed more interested in my automobile than in my friends or classes, I came to realize that he liked offering pointers about the things that he knew well. And the advice he gave me was almost always sound.

You can change. The dad I knew as a little child and even a teenager is different from the one I have now. He always loved Mom, my brother, and me, but he didn't always know how to show it. And as he will admit, he made a lot of mistakes in the way he handled his emotions. However, with the Lord's help, he has become a softer, gentler, more godly person. I am so thankful that he didn't stay the same or become bitter as he grew older.

Always carry a hanky. Our ranch was seventeen miles southeast of the nearest town. Every day during the school year (until I was old enough to drive), I rode to school with Dad. Since I have allergies, he always tucked an extra handkerchief in his suit coat. Many times on the way to town, I asked him for it. It became a family joke (Dad always had an extra handkerchief for Dena). I never even thought of getting my own because he seemed to like providing one for me.

And as I grew up, Dad provided other things for me: love, security, and money for college, to name just a few. He supported my dreams and cheered me on. Since my dreams included marriage to a godly man, Dad prayed faithfully for me to find the right person to share my life with. In 1995, when I married my best friend, my dad said he wasn't sad to give me away because he knew I was so happy (and he even turned off a Dallas Cowboys game to grant his blessing when Carey asked for my hand in marriage—talk about sacrifice).

My heart was full on my wedding day—so when I was finished getting ready in the bride's room and my dad came in to see me before the ceremony began, I started to cry. I knew I would always be "Daddy's little girl," and I was thankful for his guidance. But part of me was sad, too, that I was leaving the relative safety of childhood behind.

Suddenly, Daddy reached out his arm toward me. In his hand was a familiar object. "Need a handkerchief?" he asked. I burst out laughing.

So Dad, if you're reading this, know that I appreciate the things you've taught me, whether by design or by osmosis. There's just one thing: You can quit asking about my bank account now!

FIVE GROOVY WAYS TO SAY "I LOVE YOU" TO YOUR PARENTS

PEPPER'S PIT STOPS

1. As they grow older and it becomes harder to find a gift for them, *make* a gift. Maybe have their grandchildren create a simple scrapbook, which you can add to each year. Or create an *experience* instead by checking out what's unique to your area. You might even take them on a tour or buy them tickets to a lecture, concert, or professional sporting event.

2. Don't delay in reconciling unresolved differences. Call or e-mail them today. Although the hurts may not be resolved in one day, your efforts will prove you love them.

3. Videotape an interview with your folks. Ask them questions about their childhood, their career(s), and when and how they met. Or, ask them to e-mail you stories about specific periods in their lives. Compile the messages into a notebook and give one to each family member at Christmas.

4. Rub tired or swollen legs or backs.

5. Thank them for deciding to bring you into this world!

FAMILY REUNION

PATRICIA LORENZ

It's finally over. The last child has been delivered to the airport. The last set of sheets and towels has been washed, folded, and put away; the last of the leftovers eaten or tossed. It's really over—twelve days of houseguests culminating with three days of family reunion. *How is it,* I wonder, *that one man—Edward J. Kobbeman, fighter pilot in World War I—could get married in 1944, have three children, and end up with a family swelled to two dozen people?*

All but four of those family members stayed at my house for a long family reunion weekend. One, my oldest daughter, arrived from New York the Thursday before and stayed until the Tuesday after. My youngest son arrived from Arizona the Saturday of the reunion and stayed for ten days. But on the big weekend itself, the one we officially called "the family reunion," twenty of us gathered. Dad, Bev (our beloved step-mother since 1982), my brother, my sister, and me, three spouses, our children (eight of Dad's nine grandchildren), three of his six great-grandchildren, and one niece's boyfriend.

Half of those twenty people stayed at my house for three days or more.

They descended from sea to shining lake, from north, south, east, and west, from states near and far, in planes and in three family vans. We talked, cooked, ate, drank, ate again, looked at photo albums, cracked jokes, laughed like hyenas, played basketball, baseball, and Frisbee, and took turns holding the family's newest baby. Then Joe, my brother, out riding bikes with his wife, called on his cell phone. He was out of breath with excitement.

"Quick, tell everybody to get down here to the railroad tracks. The country's largest still-running steam locomotive is making a historic run across America and it'll be passing through in seven minutes. You'll never see this again!"

You'd have thought Christmas morning had arrived, and Joe felt certain Santa had left a new bike or his first model train, complete with a real whistle and trestle.

"Seven minutes?" I stuttered, "How can we all get there in seven minutes?"

"Just get down here! It's only a mile or so."

Well, believe it or not, the entire family raced for the vans, piled in, and got there in plenty of time. One thing about our old-fashioned American family: It doesn't take a whole lot to entertain us.

The great steam engine (and its dozen or so old-fashioned cars) zipping across America was a little late, so we waited in the hot sun by the railroad tracks, knowing full well that mighty train wouldn't slow down at the railroad crossing in our sleepy little suburb town.

We all stood around googly-eyed, staring down the railroad tracks, talking and joking as we waited for the monster and its passengers.

Dad and Joe filled us in on the details of the mighty steam engine we were about to witness. All the kids, including my nearly-fifty-year-old brother, put pennies and quarters on the tracks so the steaming beast could pulverize them into worthless pieces of metal in a split second.

Still straining our eyes to catch that first glimpse of the coming train, we joked about how this was the most excitement we'd had since the pigs got loose at the county fair—and then we put a few more pennies down on the tracks.

Finally the big black beast roared toward us from the distance, coming closer and closer, as adults whisked the grandchildren away from the tracks. And whoosh, there she was—whistles blowing, steam flowing, tracks clacking—going what seemed like warp speed and then—whoosh! Ten seconds later ... she was gone.

All the giggling kids, aged eighty-two on down, gathered our now-useless change from the weeds beside the tracks, headed back to the vans, and drove home. It had been exciting, all right. Well, maybe not *that* exciting, but we did it together as a family.

From Dad, the octogenarian head of our crew, down to three-month-old Chloe, we were simply a family waiting to watch a train fly by, then eager to get home again to finish what all families do at reunions ... talk, eat, drink, laugh, play, and, sometimes, drop everything to go make a memory. The activities don't really matter. The most important part is the gathering ... and the love.

Family. It truly is a wonderful word.

Patricia Lorenz is a speaker and author of six books, including her latest, True Pilot Stories *(InfinityPublishing). She's also a contributing writer to over two dozen* Chicken Soup for the Soul *books (HCI). Visit www.PatriciaLorenz.com.*

FAVORITE OFFBEAT ROAD TRIP EXITS

Leaning Tower of ... Texas? Next time you're on Route 66, drop by Groom, Texas, to check out their leaning water tower. What was the cause of this tipping? Hurricane? Nope. Earthquake? Nope. Prairie dog tunnels? Nope. According to legend, it was built that way on purpose, to get drivers' attention. And it worked!

The Soo Locks of Sault Ste. Marie, Michigan (near the border of Canada). What do you do when two separate bodies of water—with differing water levels—converge? Have the water and boat run through a system of locks, which changes the water level right before your eyes! Little Groovy Dudes would love to see this mechanical marvel.

PART THREE

I Wanna Hold Your Hand (Young Love)

The Groovy Chicks' Road Trip

WISHIN' AND HOPIN' AND PRAYIN' AND CRYIN'

LAURA JENSEN WALKER

EXCERPTED FROM *GIRL TIME: A CELEBRATION OF CHICK FLICKS, BAD HAIR DAYS & GOOD FRIENDS* (REVELL)

So, what did he say then?"

"He asked me if I liked ice cream and wanted to go out after singles group tonight and have some Ben & Jerry's."

"No! Really?"

"Really," I said with great anticipation.

"So he asked you out on a date!"

"D'ya think? Maybe he just likes ice cream ..."

"Did he ask anyone else to join you?"

"No ..."

"Well, then it's a date! Call me afterward and tell me everything!"

Turns out it wasn't a date after all—he was just in the mood to go get some ice cream with a friend. Heavy sigh.

Another dating hope bit the dust.

How well I remember those wishin' and hopin' and prayin'-to-meet-Mr.-Right days of singleness. Many were the times those hopes, wishes, and prayers ended up in tears—for me and for my single girlfriends.

"But I thought he *liked* me! If he didn't like me, then why'd he hold my hands at the movies and kiss me when he took me home?"

"'Cause he's a guy."

"But if it didn't mean anything to him, then why'd he do it?"

"Hormones."

"But you'd think a Christian guy would know better!"

"He's still a guy with hormones."

Being single and a Christian was a confusing business. We wanted to honor God and seek him first and not make meeting Mr. Right our focus. Yet we heard sermons all the time about the joys of marriage, and blissfully married couples surrounded us on all sides.

And you know what else? We had hormones, too.

It didn't help when guys sent us mixed signals.

"You never really knew if it was a date," my best friend Lana recalled of our time together in a large church singles group. "You weren't sure when a guy invited you to do something if he was interested in you or just doing the group-fun thing."

Several of us women in our early thirties decided that the existing single guys at church must have gone through some secret initiation. We figured any time a new single guy came into the group, the others would quickly pull him into the men's room and warn, "Now, don't sit next to a single woman at church unless you're in a big group or she'll think you want to marry her. And never, *ever* ask her to do something one-on-one or she'll start planning the wedding."

Can you say "a little over the top"? We usually didn't start planning the wedding until the guy sat next to us at least *twice*.

My friend Chuck sat by me in church all the time, so he shouldn't have been surprised when I fell for him. For three years I was not-so-secretly crazy about the tall, good-looking Chuck, whom I'd met at singles group and become good friends with. I was absolutely convinced he was THE MAN GOD HAD

CHOSEN FOR ME, only he didn't know it yet. So I was willing to be patient until he saw the light.

He never saw the light.

And I made myself alternately crazy and miserable over our "relationship," or lack thereof. It was never more than a friendship on Chuck's part, and he told me that—countless times. But when he'd smile down from his tall Norwegian bachelor position and ask me to do something, no matter what my head said—*It doesn't mean anything. He's just a friend. He's not interested in you that way*—my heart, which is a pretty strong muscle all its own, would always flutter and hope *maybe this time he'll fall.*

Lana and I, roommates at the time, would have long talks about Chuck and my feelings for him. Although she liked and respected him, I was her best friend and she didn't want to see me get hurt. So the day finally came when my wise and practical friend said, "Laura, you need to stop spending so much time with Chuck. You know he only wants to be friends, but you want more, and being around him all the time is setting yourself up for heartache and disappointment."

I acknowledged that she was right and agreed to move on and stop doing things with Chuck—the man of my dreams.

A few days after this heartfelt conversation, Lana went on a daylong singles event—which I'd declined to attend, pleading too much homework (which was true). But later that day, Chuck called and asked me to go to a matinee with him and another friend.

Guess what I did? Movie lover that I am, I couldn't refuse. It had nothing to do with Chuck. At least that's what I told Lana when she called on the way home from her outing to invite me to pizza with the gang.

I didn't understand why she got angry. She was leading with her head; I was leading with my masochistic heart.

When Chuck moved to Texas three years later, I discovered

there really was something to that old cliché "Out of sight, out of mind." Not wanting to waste any more time pining away after someone I couldn't have, for my thirty-fourth birthday I took out a personal ad in the *Pennysaver* that said, "Wanted: a Christian man who reads!"

Only problem: I forgot to read the fine print that said every time I called the 900 number to listen to the responses to my ad, I was charged thousands and thousands of pennies. When my phone bill arrived a few weeks later with more than four hundred dollars in charges, I hung up my man-hunting hat. It cost too much.

And *that's* when I decided to let God do the hunting for me. But because I'm a girl through and through, I never gave up wishin' and hopin' and prayin'.

Laura Jensen Walker is a writer, speaker, and breast-cancer survivor. She is married to Renaissance-man husband Michael and has one child: a canine "daughter" named Gracie. She resides in northern California. She loves books, show tunes, and cookies-and-cream ice cream, but hates math, rodents, and hot weather.

Yick and Double Yick

Nineteen seventy-one was a long, hard year of unrequited love. I was in seventh grade and Jeff was the boy for me. In my pubescent mind, "like-liking" Jeff filled the majority of my thoughts. The year passed without him casting even a wayward glance my way, and by eighth grade, my thoughts of ever becoming Mrs. Jeffrey Young had been tossed out along with my fishnet stockings.

Robby was my new love—at least in my dreams. I spent many a slumber party with my chums, Lilly and Cindy, going over and over that one burning question: might ... did ... could ... Robby ever like me?

But in May of my eighth grade year, a very strange thing happened. Jeff Young asked me to go steady! I said yes. But what about my undying love for Robby? I figured it would be a waste of my seventh grade year—nine long months spent trying to charm Jeff—to not take him up on his offer. (This was my first lesson in how humans of the male persuasion take FOREVER getting things!)

I became Jeff Young's girlfriend. Officially. Only one tiny problem: I didn't like him. I kept thinking the feelings would return but they didn't, so I spent my time ditching him in the school's hallway. Then the most ghastly thing began happening when I couldn't dodge him, and he walked me to my next class. Before I stepped through the doorway, he surrounded me with his arms, and leaned in to try to kiss me. Yick!

Each time, I ducked swiftly under his outstretched arms. He tried again and again at different times, always with the same response from me, until I thought for sure he'd get the message. (Don't ask why I didn't just break up with him ... who can reason with a teenager, anyway?)

But one day, when he walked me to the corner of a loud, busy intersection where we were to split off in different directions, I leaned toward Jeff to say good-bye. Apparently, I got too close—because he grabbed my arms and laid a big, wet kiss on me. Double yick!!!

I said good-bye quickly. With every step of the two mile walk home, I got more and more grossed out at the thought of what happened. I rubbed my lips raw with the back of my hand and tried to gather saliva to spit, but most of us girls just aren't good spitters. That icky feeling just wouldn't go away.

I knew what I had to do. The walk home took forever, but when I finally arrived, I went straight to the bathroom and washed my mouth out with soap. Oh, the horrid taste … but ah, the cleansing!

So that's the story of my first kiss, and how real Dove— I mean, love—didn't find me until I was older, wiser, and smarter. And it's 99.44 percent purely true.

DEAD-END ROAD REDEMPTION

TIFFANY COMBS

After being dumped on a dead-end road, I never tired of coming up with ways to tell my friends it was over between my boyfriend and me. Some of my favorites: "Yeah, well … we had really just come to the end of the road, you know?" and "We felt the need to take a different direction." You get the picture. Though later I enjoyed the irony of being dumped by my first love on a literal dead-end road, I assure you it wasn't a laughing matter at the time. We had been dating for five splendid months. At seventeen years old, I had never been so in love. He and I had met the summer before when I was working at Subway, my very first job. By the time we met, I had already acquired the distinguished title of "sandwich artist."

This title intrigued me. Prior to being employed there, I hadn't realized that sandwich making was one of the art forms. As I passed the hours baking bread, filling up the ice machine, and selling gooey chocolate chip cookies, I couldn't help but wonder if there were entire museums somewhere dedicated to the art of sandwich making. Would I, in time, be skilled enough to have one of my very own sandwich creations entombed in a glass case for the world to admire? I imagined one of those sophisticated gold plates resting beside my sandwich. It would read, "The BLT, by Tiffany Combs. Please do not touch ... or eat."

One afternoon, immersed in grandiose thoughts of becoming a world-renowned "sandwich artist," I looked up to take the next customer's order and found myself face-to-face with the guy of my dreams. He had a quarterback build, brown hair, and kind eyes. Instantly, every attempt at impressing him with my sandwich-making skills became foiled. Deciphering between all of those fresh green vegetables can be terribly confusing when a girl finds herself falling in love with the man across the counter.

Throughout the remainder of the summer, I anxiously watched for him to come in the door—and to my delight, he often did. I attribute his being attracted to me to the stylish black visor I wore. I believe the melodramatic soft-rock tunes playing in the background deserve some credit, as well. After all, how could he *not* fall in love with Michael Bolton, Whitney Houston, and Lionel Ritchie belting out their best ballads from the seventies, eighties, and nineties?

From the very beginning, our conversations across the sneeze guard were deep and soul-searching.

"White or wheat?"

"Um, I'll have white please."

"Six inch or footlong?

"Six inch."

"Cheese?"

"Yes."

"American or Swiss?"

"American is fine."

By the end of the summer, I had learned intimate details about him, such as whether or not he preferred mayonnaise, mustard, or creamy Italian. Despite our conversational limits, it wasn't long before we discovered we were meant for each other. Though our initial conversations were strictly sandwich-related, I discovered that much in the way of love can be said with one's smile. And his spoke volumes.

He smiled at me almost as if asking a question. An inquisitive confidence lurked behind that smile.

He must have heard a resounding "yes" when I smiled back at him over that counter. He continued to survive the summer on six-inch ham sandwiches, and several months later we ran into one another at a local basketball game. By the time the final buzzer had sounded, we had exchanged numbers and made plans for our first date.

We spent every possible moment of the next five months together. When not together in person, we spoke on the phone or over the Internet, instant-messaging "sweet nothings" across the World Wide Web. He took me to his prom, I took him to mine; I watched his baseball games, he watched my dance competitions; we played video games (which he always "let me win" even though I strongly protested); and in the car together, we sang each song on the radio at the top of our lungs. We especially enjoyed harmonizing to Patrick Swayze's "She's Like the Wind." I felt convinced he thought I was just like the wind too— whatever that meant.

All the glories of romantic love had finally arrived for my consumption. From day one my friends and family knew I was crazy about him. They said whenever I talked about him, the corners of my mouth would slowly turn up into a smile— completely against my will.

The not-so-easily communicated part of my love story is this: I knew deep down in my spirit that somewhere between "white or wheat?" and "I love you," I had made the decision to let go of God's hand and take off down the journey of first love without his guidance. Who needs the love of God when a boy thinks you're like the wind? Or, really, who even *wants* the love of God when it cautions you against such reckless abandonment to another human being? I certainly didn't.

It wasn't until my boyfriend left for summer football camp that I began to heed the uneasiness growing in my spirit. Ironically, while he was being tackled by burly Oklahoma linebackers, my own linebackers pummeled me at home. Only mine went by the names of Loneliness and Guilt.

Loneliness tackled me first because, for the first time in five months, I was without my security. Guilt came next. He hit me the hardest.

Bruised and broken, I began to realize the error of my way. I knew I had traded in the love of God for the love of a human being, and that I had broken the heart of God.

It sobered me to realize that the quality of my human relationships didn't matter when I sacrificed the quality of my relationship with God. God gently reminded me that any love that has become a substitute for his divine love is really no love at all, and however painful a process, such love must be given back to him.

So that's what I did. With soaked eyes and a face that no longer curled in an instantaneous smile, I surrendered my boyfriend to God. I entrusted the relationship to his loving care, regardless of what such care might require. In fact, I count it a blessing that I did not know the implications of such a reckless surrender—for I might never have uttered those words.

My boyfriend came home from camp the next week and broke up with me. We spent nearly four hours parked on that dead-end road, nestled way back in the arms of the lake. As we talked, we watched the sun set and the night introduce the stars one by one. He said that though he'd like to explain why he had to break up with me, he couldn't. He just suddenly knew he needed to end our relationship.

I didn't need him to explain. I knew the reason for our breakup was bigger than both of us. I'd arrived on that dead-end road because of the love of someone else—someone who had heard my prayer of repentance and surrender and responded faithfully; painfully, but faithfully.

In my quest for true love, God has continued to confront me with dead-end road signs. I am grateful my Father has allowed me to get my heart broken by boys who smile kindly at me from across counters. From such heartache I've learned the limits of human love. I've learned the hard way that God often asks me to give up that which is good for that which is better—his love and approval.

Any search for love which doesn't start off with God brings me to the same place—the middle of nowhere. There, I confront the telltale road signs, and let my tears of disappointment and disillusionment fall and darken the dusty road around me.

And there I am assured that it isn't my desire for love that's wrong, but simply the road I traveled in search of it. The only road worth traveling is the one on which the love of God is the treasure I'm seeking. And to be sure, this road does *not* have a dead end.

Tiffany Combs is originally from Chandler, Oklahoma. She attended Oklahoma Baptist University, where she received a degree in Family Psychology. She is currently living in Waco, Texas, and studying at Baylor University's Truett Seminary.

STARSHINE'S HOW'S YOUR INNERSTATE?

THOUGHTS ON MARRIAGE

Questions for Reflection and Journaling

☺ Do you believe God has a specific person in mind for each of us to marry? Why or why not?

☺ If you are married, what drew you to your spouse? If you are single and would like to be married, what qualities do you feel are important in a mate?

☺ Are there couples in your life whom you admire? What about in your church or community? What specific things do you appreciate about their relationship?

☺ For further reflection, spend some time looking at couples in scripture (Abraham and Sarah, Ruth and Boaz, etc.) with the help of biblical commentaries and the Holy Spirit. See what God might teach you through their examples.

A BABE IN BOYLAND

NANCY C. ANDERSON

I squealed with joy as happy tears splashed on my go-go boots. The Beatles were on the *Ed Sullivan Show,* and I watched with enraptured bliss. I was in love with Paul McCartney—and I *knew* that somehow, some way, he would find and marry me. Though only in the fourth grade at the time, I was an optimist.

But while I waited for Paul to come searching for me in Winona, Minnesota, I found a stand-in. Already the cutest boy in class, Jack walked into class one day with a Beatle haircut and captivated me. But I didn't know how to approach Jack, one of the cool kids, because I was only average—in every way except one: I was an excellent schemer.

One morning, Jack got in trouble for passing a note to Wendy (another cool kid—she owned a horse), and the teacher sentenced him to after-school detention. That meant he would have to clean all the chalkboard erasers in the entire school. *Aha,* I thought, *here's my chance.* I behaved obnoxiously for the rest of the day until I earned my detention.

Jack and I went from room to room, asking the teachers for their blackboard erasers. Then we took them into the janitor's closet and fed them into a cleaning machine. With each grinding, swishing sound, with each breath of chalk dust, I fell deeper in love. When his hand brushed against mine, I thought I would faint. He started to talk to me as if I was cool, and suddenly, I was. The next day, he gave me a note containing the deepest, most meaningful words I had ever read: "I like you."

Our romance lasted for several months, until I outgrew him and developed a killer crush on a sixth grader who looked like Davy Jones of The Monkees.

The summer between sixth and seventh grade, I gave my first kiss to my neighbor, Billy. Well ... actually, he bought it from me.

I was working outside, pulling weeds in my front yard when Billy careened around the corner on his red Stingray bike. He skidded to a stop in front of me and said, "I got you somethin'." Then he held up a little stuffed animal—a mouse.

Billy said, "I heard you tell my sister that you wanted this ... that you'd do just about anything to get it, so I bought it from her. I'll give it to ya—for a kiss." Without a hint of hesitation, I leaned over the bike, kissed him full on the lips, grabbed the mouse, and ran. We both got what we wanted—fair trade.

My next little caper didn't go as well. By the time I reached high school, I was crazy in love with Jimmy. I wrote him poem after poem. He said I was a great writer and, of course, I believed him. But secretly, I wondered if I could keep writing such epic poetry. I was slowly but surely running out of words that rhymed with kiss.

One day, while sitting on my bed trying to think of a non-offensive rhyme for heart, I heard a breathtaking song on an old Peter, Paul, and Mary album. The lyrics were haunting. My devious mind kicked into high gear and developed a plan: *He'll never know I didn't write it. He would never listen to an album by folksingers. He's a rock 'n' roll guy—I can get away with it.* I wrote down the first verse to the song, and signed my name to it.

Jimmy was amazed at my new creation. He said, "I think you could sell this, it's really, really good!"

I explained, "You were my inspiration, it just says how I feel about you—about us."

A week later, I was riding in the car with my mother when a DJ announced the title of a new hit single. I froze. That was the name of *my* poem! The deep, rich voice of Roberta Flack sang, "The first time ever I saw your face—I thought the sun rose in your eyes...."

Jimmy never spoke to me again.

My scheming had backfired. However, I didn't fully learn my lesson until several years later, after I married Ron, my college sweetheart. Even though I had become a Christian, I was still selfish and manipulative—and a terrible wife. Only after I nearly lost my marriage did I realize that the road to love is not a one-way street.

So I asked the Lord to help me to put his love into action, and I began to live the verse in 1 Corinthians 13:5, "[Love] is not rude, it is not self-seeking." I learned to find joy in serving others and looked for ways to help my husband accomplish his goals. He, in turn, helped me accomplish mine. We are now walking down Lovers Lane as a team, holding hands, side-by-side.

Next year we will celebrate our twenty-eighth anniversary—and the only thing I'm scheming about now is how to surprise him with a trip to Hawaii.

Nancy C. Anderson is an author and speaker who lives in southern California with her husband of twenty-seven years and their teenage son. For more info on her writing, speaking, or marriage ministry visit www.NancyCAnderson.com.

STARSHINE'S SMILE MARKERS

Love makes a good eye squint.
GEORGE HERBERT

THE PORK CHOP

JINNY HENSON

S cientists discovered recently that being in love produces the equivalent of an amphetamine-induced high. I realize after ten years of marriage that no human would voluntarily make this commitment unless they were smoking crack. Which leads me to this conclusion: God is pretty smart.

I'd tried blind dates. You go to be polite and learn you have as much in common with the guy as with the Unabomber. But my parents met on one and who was I to resist fate, should it choose to repeat itself? I'm no obsessive-compulsive, but when you're a girl dealing with something as serious as love, you have to touch every light switch twice and avoid the cracks in the ground or you might just miss "the one."

There was the relationship with the English major who insisted we double-date with other English majors. They would form a conversational trinity discussing Thoreau and why he went into the woods. Conversely, I, the intellectual Pee Wee Herman, sat pondering questions like, "In *One Fish, Two Fish, Red Fish, Blue Fish*, why was the fish red? What made him so blue?"

During my junior year in college, I felt convinced God would give me either Steve or Mike for a husband—and I generously told him I didn't really care either way. He could have the final answer as to which one I would grow old and wrinkly with. Strangely enough, summer approached and they both graduated, having somehow forgotten to fall madly in love with me. Since I had not even dated either of them, I have no idea why this surprised me.

So maybe I wasn't so lucky at love. But, as I rifled through and discarded romances as if searching for the perfect prom dress, I just *knew* I was on the right track. My mother accused me of being too picky. But I didn't want someone with incorrect grammar raising my children. Or someone who held his fork the wrong way. Or someone who expected *me*, in all of my Southern belle glory, to actually PAY for my dinner. I knew she feared that my ship would never come in, but I had hunkered down with my fat beach umbrella and a cold Diet Coke—in zestful expectation.

Call it anticipation. Just the thought that Mr. Right could be behind me in the Cinnabon line thrilled me to no end. I was on the cusp of big things and more ready than an Atkins dieter at an all-you-can-eat omelet bar.

But the anticipation ebbed and flowed as seminary pumped theology into my brain. Not such a hot crowd there. The field was rife with full-grown men wearing flood pants and carrying tote bags. However, I had determined to never marry a preacher, so I wasn't *that* concerned. I intended to get my master's degree and head off to Atlanta to work for the Olympics. I'd hatched that plan with a friend at CNN.

Besides, I was the bungee-jumping type. No holiness bun for this girl. I was a pork chop—with no desire to be squeezed into a Jell-O mold. Even if you blended the thing up and mixed it with Knox Gelatin, it still wouldn't firm up.

See, I was never prim and proper and certainly didn't soak in any of that "personality" at seminary. For example, my theology professor, Calvin Miller, began the semester's brilliant discourse: "Jeremiah ..."

"Was a bullfrog?" I interjected. Oh, I was so proud of myself.

I looked normal enough on the outside, but my innards blazed with wild dreams that no life as a preacher's wife could hope to accommodate. I was quirky, too, giving no thought to stapling a hem that needed fixing, spray-painting my shoes a new color, or trimming my own hair at midnight. My parents raised me to believe that anything was possible—whether it be house painting or do-it-yourself dentistry.

I thought life to be one grand experiment—and the minister's wife petri dish was something I would pass on.

Then a shoe changed my life forever. I glanced down in Sunday school (a messed-up name for a place where *adults* go, if you ask me), and saw a rather good-looking shoe. My dad had been a men's clothing manager for Neiman Marcus and Saks, so I knew a nice shoe when I saw one.

"Oh, I love your shoes!" I gushed to the owner in my filterless way.

"Thank you," he replied politely, with a furrowed brow.

"They remind me of my dad," I emoted, head cocked respectfully with a pout as I thought of my sweet daddy.

He now looked at me as though I were nursing an octopus.

Shoe boy had a name: John. No tote bag either, I noticed as I flitted from class to class. He noticed my raucous laughter across campus. "There goes that crazy blonde," he'd say.

But I had no second thoughts because I was never going to ever be a preacher's wife. (Okay. Watch—this is funny. Tell God what you don't want in life and see where it gets you.)

It just so happened that John was studying to be a pastor. As I would see him studying in the library or hear him ask for prayer for his mom who had cancer, I began having troubling thoughts about his dark hair, discreet sense of humor, and the fire in his belly. This awesome guy made Steve and Mike look like Napoleon Dynamite.

It made me bitter to realize that the best bakery in town just opened on a street I had forbidden myself to walk down. Darn that carrot cake! Just what was God up to? John asked me out ... and paid. He was funny, irreverent, holy, and smart. *And* going to be a pastor? I didn't know they came in this flavor.

Since Jesus is all about the "follow my will" thing, I knew I had to pray about this ... and quickly. Could this be my life? Could I really live in a parsonage and have seventeen children named things like Zechariah and Shekinah? I didn't think so. But this man was so incredible. I could tell he accepted me, even in my most random moments. He even seemed smitten by my spunk. I couldn't help but think that he liked me now— but what about when I taught the children to rap at Vacation Bible School and the board garnished his wages?

My father in his infinite wisdom had a solution to my quandary: "Reel him into the boat, Jinny, and if you don't like him you can always throw him back." That innocent statement helped me turn a corner, and I knew from that day on I would have to learn to be the preacher's wife.

Listen, I got shanghaied, pure and simple. The old switch-a-roo. We were engaged four months later and married a year after that. We finished seminary together. In ten years, we've had two kids and two parents' funerals, owned four houses, and started two churches. The dreams I'd convinced myself that no pastor's-wife-life would allow have come true. John is proud of his wife, the stand-up comedian.

Only in God's economy can what we fear the most become the treasure we would choose never to live without.

Jinny Henson is a stand-up comedian who's performed in comedy clubs and churches across the country. Her favorite roles, however, are those of John's wife, Maggie Lee and Jack's mom, and sinner saved by grace.

GROOVLARATIONS!

Groov/lar/a/tion: n. A declaration or description of something monumentally Groovy, derived by combining two or more words.

Some of my favorite Pit Stops are at Groovy Chicks' book signings, where we get to meet you, our readers! At Pepper's very first book release party, we celebrated by having a Groovlaration contest! These were some of our best entries …

Extraordinarilicious: Over and above the common; wonderfully flavorful. —Deb Meyer, Maitland, Florida

Narlydacious: Awesomely beautiful man. —Yvonne Rice, Longwood, Florida

Chicktagious: Anyone drawn to pink, glitter, and other "foo-foo" items. —Kerrie Stumpf and Maria Lee, Winter Springs, Florida

Menosaurus: A woman beyond menopause. —Alanna Hogan, Chuluota, Florida

These just crack me up! Send your own groovlarations (word and definition) to pepper@groovychicksroadtrip.com. We'll put our favorites on our Web site or possibly in our next book!

FOR BETTER OR FERWERDA

JULIE FERWERDA

(ORIGINALLY PUBLISHED IN

MARRIAGE PARTNERSHIP, SPRING 2005)

D o you, Steve, take this woman, and do you, Julie, take this man, to be your lawfully wedded spouse, to have and to hold, for better or for worse, in sickness and in health, in constant reminders and helpful suggestions, in specific details, step-by-step instructions, and redundant directions, as long as you both shall live?"

Those weren't our wedding vows—but they should have been. This became apparent a few weeks into our marriage. An afternoon bike ride turned ugly when Steve had the nerve to correct my technique—as if I didn't know how to ride a bike.

I was pedaling along, daydreaming about my wonderful husband, sure that at any moment he'd pull off the path and sneak a kiss. My lips were practically puckered with anticipation when he said, "You need to shift down."

"What?" I asked, not sure I heard him correctly.

"You're in too high a gear for this hill," he panted. "Shift down a couple."

I bristled with indignation. "I *know* about gear shifting; I'm not an idiot. And don't tell me what to do."

We didn't speak for the rest of the ride.

Later, after we apologized—and he offered to do the dinner dishes—I walked into the kitchen and stared in shock.

"Steve, that won't work," I told him as I approached the dishwasher and began to undo what he'd done. "The plates go on this rack, the saucers go here, and if you don't turn the silverware *this* way, they won't get clean. Oh, and did you remember to spray the sponge with antibacterial soap?"

In the following weeks it wasn't uncommon for one of us to say things such as, "How did I ever get my driver's license?"; "I can't believe I survived in this world for thirty-three years without you"; "You apparently think *Computers for Dummies* was written with me in mind"; and "Remind me not to talk so I won't say the wrong thing." Our insecurities grew.

Finally, one evening we went out to eat with some friends. Three-quarters into my salad, Steve—who knew I was trying to lose weight—grabbed the plate and said loud enough for the surrounding tables to hear, "Honey, don't you think you've had enough?" Feeling all eyes upon my beet-red face, I answered sweetly, "Yes, definitely! How nice of you to remind me to save room for dessert. I think I'll have that triple brownie deluxe sundae."

"We need to talk," I told him when we returned home. "It hurts when you criticize the way I do things."

"Well, what about the constant advice you pile on?" he said. "I feel inadequate when you tell me your way is better. It seems as if I can't do anything right."

There it finally was—out in the open: Our need for control had gotten out of control.

We decided to take some serious steps to change. And that meant a lot of tongue-biting when we'd see the other doing something "wrong."

I'd cringe as I'd watch him load the dishwasher the wrong

way—but I wasn't allowed to interfere. And Steve discovered it was better for him just to leave the room rather than be tempted to look over my shoulder and correct my efforts on the computer. That's when something amazing happened: I found that the dishes still got clean. And Steve discovered I could handle projects without him.

"Okay, I admit it," I told Steve one day. "There's more than just my way to do something."

As we've granted more trust and permission to fail, our abilities and our confidence in each other have grown. We've learned to respect each other's choices.

While we still occasionally catch each other in the micromanaging act, we make light of it, with a wink and a smile, knowing that we really do love each other.

And now, it's time for me to step aside. My husband is waiting to proofread my writing for any mistakes.

Julie Ferwerda is managing editor of Young Believers in Christ Magazine *and has written for magazines such as* Discipleship Journal. *Besides managing each other, she and her husband enjoy traveling and long walks. Visit www.JulieFerwerda.com.*

STARSHINE'S SMILE MARKERS

Love is an act of endless forgiveness,
a tender look which becomes a habit.
        PETER USTINOV

JOY FOR THE BROKENHEARTED

CAROLE SUZANNE JACKSON
(ORIGINALLY APPEARED IN *LIGHT AND LIFE*
MAGAZINE, MARCH/APRIL 2006)

When Don served me marijuana-laced brownies one week before our wedding date, my world shook. My alarm heightened further when Don described how amphetamines had helped him battle depression. He stopped using speed only because his supplier cut him off.

In the two years we dated, I'd learned about substance abuse in his distant past. Now, I saw a different person—a guy who had abused drugs on and off since high school and still believed them acceptable for managing stress.

After seeking guidance from our premarital counselor, I knew what I had to do. I stood before Don and squared my shoulders to brace myself for the conversation. "We can't get married like this. You need to get help. Let's work through this first."

His eyes flashed in anger. "You've been influenced by your friends."

I glared back. "You fed me marijuana brownies knowing I hate substance abuse!"

"I messed up. It won't happen again." He pleaded and looked deep into my eyes.

"You can't promise to quit using illegal drugs. I can't trust you."

"I won't wait." His voice quivered.

"You leave me no choice. Please, work through this," I said, caressing his hand and returning his tearful gaze.

"Don't leave," he whispered, and drew me closer. Though I could feel his chest heave with sorrow, fear of a bad marriage and refusal to consider divorce as an option helped me hold my decision.

Two days before the set date, I officially called off my wedding. Nothing in life seemed as fulfilling without Don.

I'd given up my apartment and financial stability. Don would have been the main source of income during the start of our marriage and my first year of college enrollment.

Though mourning, I could still imagine Don's warmth and tender kisses. I could almost hear his laughter. These recollections mixed with the taste of gut-wrenching tears.

On our wedding date, I wished I could sleep forever. My would-be maid of honor, Kathy, called to check on me. She knew Mom and Dad were giving me time to regroup before they came to town.

Kathy offered the nudge I needed to get out of the house: horse riding. The autumn sun warmed my skin and a cool breeze caressed my hair as we navigated narrow paths in single file. Instead of the expected fragrance of wedding flowers and Don's cologne intertwined with my perfume, bottlebrush pine scent filled the air. My jean-clad knees pressed the saddle while my form-fitting white satin gown graced a closet. Horses' hooves thudded as I longed to stride in cadence to the "Wedding March." Kathy clutched her horse's bridle reins and followed me; I preferred that she'd have led me down the church aisle with bridal flowers in hand. I agonized, not knowing Don's whereabouts or mental state.

Though praising God felt foreign in that wilderness of soul,

I knew the power of pondering God's attributes. Memorized Scriptures helped me form prayers: "Your joy, Holy Lord, is my strength. You will never leave me nor forsake me. You are worthy to be praised apart from feelings. I adore you."

As my emotional pain intensified, I strained to consider God's goodness. I recollected past situations when I'd prayed through anxiety into peace. As the horse jostled along the trail, I decided to obey Hebrews 10:23: "Let us hold unswervingly to the hope we profess, for he who promised is faithful." My anguish began to give way as I grabbed hold of hope.

I started to sense God surrounding me. The movement of the horse rocked me in the saddle. The cloudless sky proclaimed God on his throne. I acknowledged him as tender and sweet to comfort me, yet strong to meet my needs.

Slowly, my determination gave way to a twinge of elation. What a surprise when childlike exuberance bubbled. *This must be the "joy of the Lord" described in the Bible,* I thought. The Holy Spirit transformed me.

Fits of uncontrollable weeping did resurface in the coming months. And whenever my resolve to draw close to God weakened, the temptation to dwell on my difficulties strengthened.

But when I chose to focus on God, joy often emerged. Corrie ten Boom's war stories inspired me to go to that place where God's children rise above the horrors life hands them. She had lost everything when Nazis invaded Holland, yet she could say, "There is no pit so deep that God is not deeper still."

God used my ordeal to secure his strength in me and develop deeper intimacy between us. So many marvels transpired as a result of prayer. Multiple provisions—housing, finance, and employment—proved God was my source.

When we face possible devastation, two choices surface— misery or faith. We can give up on life emotionally and sometimes physically or we can choose life from God.

God gives each of us a measure of faith: "Let us fix our eyes on Jesus, the author and perfecter of our faith" (Heb. 12:2). "Now faith is being sure of what we hope for and certain of what we do not see" (Heb. 11:1).

Two years passed before my general sense of normalcy returned. I will always wonder what became of Don. He refused to restore contact with our mutual friends or with me.

For comfort, I sometimes imagined resting my head in Father God's lap as though I were a small child. In staying God-focused through prayer, praise, and thanksgiving, my attitude changed from fear and sorrow to faith. Healing resulted.

Supportive friends and family also brought comfort by listening and caring. Though my mother has never shared my faith, she made a comment that impacted me greatly. Mom said, "Your God has always cared for you. He will make a way now." Perhaps I'm more useful to God now than I would have been had I lived happily ever after. The adventure of being deeply in love expanded my understanding of relationships, and the healing process sensitized me to the needs of others. As a result, I can better rejoice with those who rejoice and weep with those who weep.

Now, years later, through many successes and disappointments, life goes richly forward with the living God—who brings victory in defeat and joy in trials as I exercise the faith he has given me.

Carole Suzanne Jackson is a freelance writer, speaker, and entrepreneur. She taught Public Speaking at Valencia Community College for four years prior to working full-time as a freelancer.

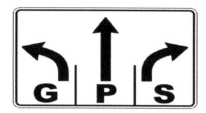

LOST? TRY GPS
(GOD'S POSITIONING SYSTEM)

"For I know the plans I have for you,"
says the LORD.
"They are plans for good and not for disaster,
to give you a future and a hope."
JEREMIAH 29:11 NLT

LOVE ON THE ROAD

DENA DYER

The first person I met at the audition was a young, eager tenor named Carey. He was one of the college grads vying for a spot in a Christian music group that would travel the country. I thought that he, a Tennessee-born-and-bred boy, was a little too friendly. After all, during my last year of college I'd sworn off men and dedicated myself to finding God's will for my life.

When Carey first met me, he thought I was cute, but a little too "Texan." Maybe it was the denim dress, cowboy boots, and jacket covered with western motifs. (What was I thinking?)

Despite the western clothing, I made the group. And Carey did too. By the second week of the tour, he and I were placed together as prayer partners. We stayed up late, talking and finding out just how much we had in common. It was sort of uncanny, actually—we had similar goals, family backgrounds, and political beliefs. We liked the same authors, movies, and jokes. And strangely enough, we had both sworn off dating until after our two-year commitment to the group.

From that point on, we were almost inseparable ... and I was hopelessly and madly in love. I had quickly done a 180-degree turn on my earlier decision to "put dating on hold" until after the tour. That just *couldn't* have been *God* telling me that! I mean, Carey was perfect—he was godly, cute, thoughtful, smart, funny, and he sang like a dream.

The only problem? Carey hadn't done a 180 and wasn't looking for a girlfriend ... not then, and maybe not for a long time. When we went out to eat, he'd say things like, "I wonder if I'll ever get married. After all, when we get off this tour, I'm going to be twenty-four—that's pretty old! And I'll still have to find a girl, get to know her, date her, and that's going to take a while. I may be thirty before I get married!"

I would look at him with a dumb smile on my face and think, *Hello! Over here! Can't you see that I'm supposed to have your babies?* But I never said a thing, because a good Texas gal knows that when a girl makes the first move, it "just ain't ladylike."

And then there was that time in the restaurant. "Wow!" Carey exclaimed. "That waitress is cute! I'd ask her out if we were in town longer!"

I felt my hand tighten around my steak knife. (Definitely *not* ladylike!)

Afterwards, I'd go to my hotel room, cry and pray, and then call my mom the next day wailing, "He doesn't even see me as a girl. I'm just his buddy!"

She'd console me by saying, "We'll just pray about it. If it's God's will, he'll come around."

For eleven months, we spent nearly every waking moment of the day together ... and I ached every second. I just *knew* he was the one for me, and I couldn't understand why he hadn't figured out that I was perfect for him. We even sang well together. What more could you want?

I often prayed for God's comfort and wisdom. And though it was a difficult time, I felt that at the very least, God was showing me that there were men in the world who were not shallow, insensitive, stuck-up, or career-driven. In other words, Carey was a good indicator that the good ones weren't all taken.

So I waited. Nothing will make you insane quite like learning patience! So I listened to Chicago's *Greatest Hits* CD and wrote in my journal as I swallowed the lump in my throat, while Carey read *Far Side* cartoons and flirted with the ski instructor we met on our day off. How in the world could he think about anyone but me?

Finally, after going through a few hundred tissues and a biblical word study on *helpmate,* I decided to stop being miserable, simply enjoy my friendship with Carey, and not let my worries about the future control my life.

So I prayed, and once again gave God control over my social life. I felt hopeful but uncertain when I went to bed that night. Looking back, I see that God was teaching me to trust him even when I couldn't see what the future held.

Nothing happened for several more months, but suddenly, Carey began treating me differently. And then one night after a concert, he asked me to walk with him to a nearby truck stop (not that romantic, but you take what you can get when you're on the road). When he told me he was having "strong feelings" about me, I nearly spit out my hot chocolate!

"Really?" I asked, my hands shaking. It's what I had longed to hear for almost a year. I couldn't quite grasp it.

"Really," he said. "I'm hoping you feel the same way."

Well, duh! I thought. But I calmly said, "Actually, I've been feeling that way for a while." And we were safely engaged before I told him the whole story—just to make *sure* he would continue thinking of me as a lady.

I know not every "I liked him, but he didn't like me" story has such a happy ending. In fact, after ten years of marriage, I can honestly say that it's not always paradise. Some days, he's my charming, romantic soulmate—and then on other days, he's more like a guy you'd meet at ... well, a truck stop. But the God who placed us in that singing group is the very one who keeps us singing in harmony ... at least about the stuff that really matters.

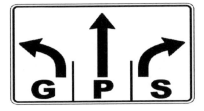

Lost? Try GPS
(God's Positioning System)

Be devoted to one another in brotherly love. Honor one
another above yourselves.
ROMANS 12:10

PART FOUR

GOIN' TO THE CHAPEL (Mature Love)

ENCOUNTER

JEANNE LEMAY

I hate being a beginner. Like a wallflower at her first seventh-grade dance, I feel self-conscious, awkward, and nervous. Yet my heart longs to dance, to feel the empowerment of gliding across the dance floor with an air of confidence like Cinderella dancing with Prince Charming. I've been yearning to learn ballroom dancing for a lifetime.

Finally, when the opportunity arrives, mixed emotions confront me. In this, the winter of my life, gravity has taken its toll. I more closely resemble the ugly stepsister than Cinderella. I'm too hardened to learn ballroom dancing. Yet my heart is still that of a young woman yearning for my very own Cinderella experience.

I glance at my Prince Charming. Like Jack Benny, he's been celebrating his thirty-ninth birthday for decades now. What's left of his hair is gray. His hands and his morale are worn from a lifetime of work. His soft belly now replaces the firm abs of his youth. For both of us, our marriage has been a disappointment. One strained day turned into months; months turned into years. Out of obligation or habit or one last hope, we agreed to try ballroom dancing.

We arrived at the dance studio just as the teacher assembled the women for the first lesson. "Ladies on the dance floor," began the graceful, confident instructor. My self-conscious stance began to wane as the lesson started, because every ounce of my concentration was consumed with figuring out where to place my feet.

After the teacher demonstrated the basic footwork, she told us to stand on the sidelines and observe the gentlemen. As they moved to the dance floor, I discreetly focused a critical eye on my husband. I did not want to be embarrassed by his awkwardness. To my relief, he fit in. He was no worse and no better than the others.

Week after week, we both methodically learned the pattern of the footwork. Then it was time to practice our individual parts—together. "Gentlemen, take a partner," the instructor announced, "and face your lady with your right hand providing the lead and support for your dance 'framework.' Don't worry about the lead yet. Just concentrate on your basic footwork as you practice with your partner. Your ability to lead will come ... eventually. Then you will be dancing as a couple, and you'll be proud to show off your lady as the centerpiece."

Apprehension showed in my husband's eyes.

"Couples, assume proper dance position," the teacher continued. "Make sure you have 'tone' as a couple. Tone is the exertion of light pressure toward your partner through your arms and upper body. Each of you will maintain your own tone or individuality, yet your partner needs to be sensitive to your every move. Gentlemen, you are not to force your partner nor are you to push or yank her. Rather, you gently give the lead with assertive movements on her backbone with your arm. Ladies, the man initiates the lead; you are to simply respond graciously by practicing the movements you have learned."

"Ladies, be patient," the instructor continued. "Men have a lot of responsibility and a lot to learn at once. Your job is to be a gracious 'follower.' Beware of 'back leading'—telling your man what to do and how to do it."

Our attempts to dance were strained, awkward, and uncomfortable. As we drove home in silence, I kept thinking we were less Cinderella and Prince Charming than Archie and Edith Bunker. I suddenly felt sad, disappointed, and discouraged.

We have a long way to go in the dance of life, I thought.

I persevered through the beginner's stage of lessons despite a constant deluge of negative feelings. I had made a commitment, and I was determined to keep my word. I found the footwork to be easy; however, I struggled against the constant temptation of back leading (nagging). To avoid failure—which my pride would not allow—I focused on mastering my role as "gracious partner." My pride would not allow me to fail.

Week by week my husband and I persisted faithfully until we actually began to enjoy ourselves.

One evening, I envisioned another partner interrupting us. My husband's face faded, and I felt the Holy Spirit impress upon me that Jesus was now my partner. As we entered dance position, his power and confidence overwhelmed my entire being and chased away all awareness of my surroundings. He led me gracefully and purposefully across the dance floor, and soon all of my inhibitions, inadequacies, and self-consciousness vanished. As I relaxed in his presence and embrace, I could see nothing but his beautiful face. His voice was music to my ears, and his words mesmerized me.

I felt like Cinderella at last.

He began to teach me. "As you dance with your life partner, Beloved, I want you to consider your conduct. Are you gentle with him? Are you faithful to encourage him when his footwork is not perfect? Do you affirm his efforts and improvement? Or do you cause strife and dissension with your critical attitude? Is your joy based only on his performance? Are you prideful?

"Is your tone patient and kind? Do you relate unconditional love to your partner? Do you submit to his lead with respect, or do you constantly try to lead for him?

"As your two hearts become one, does your countenance reflect that union? Does the dance bring you love, joy, and peace?" With those questions ringing in my ear, my Prince Charming disappeared, and I saw again my husband's face. I danced the last dance with him in silent humility.

That night as I lay awake, reflecting on the encounter until the wee hours of the morning, I was convicted of my sins, which had contributed to the demise of our marriage. Warm tears stung my eyes as I crawled out of bed and fell to my knees.

"God, I've been so wrong," I said. "I've blamed my husband for everything. I've been critical, unforgiving, nagging, uncompromising, and selfish. Please forgive me! Make me the helpmate and partner you created me to be. Teach me your virtues and replace my sins with the fruit of your Spirit. Make me a wife worthy of my husband's love."

As I wept, I felt the comfort of a warm hand as my partner gently wiped my tears and lifted me into his arms. "May I have this dance?" he asked.

And so we began a new dance together, two becoming one. He mastered the lead and covered me with his protective love. I learned to submit and respond with gracious respect. For the first time in years, I saw him with renewed eyes and heart.

I truly am Cinderella, and he is forever my Prince Charming.

Jeanne LeMay is a pseudonym for a freelance writer from Orlando, Florida, who enjoys encouraging women by writing stories based on personal struggles. She is currently working on a book to help Christian women in emotionally abusive marriages. She may be contacted at jeannelemay@bellsouth.com.

GET AWAY

Excerpted from
I Love You … Still (Revell)
by Martha Bolton

Countless couples on the brink of separation have saved their marriages by attending marriage seminars or retreats. Even more couples have gone simply to give their marriage a tune-up—a refresher course.

Getting away from the kids, the phone, the in-laws, and the bills, and focusing solely on your partner can give your marriage a brand-new perspective. But how do you know when it's time for you and your spouse to go on a marriage retreat? The following checklist might help.

You know it's time for a marriage retreat when:

☺ You set the table and he's the only one who gets a paper plate.

☺ Lately, the family dog has been getting better cuts of meat than you.

☺ All week long he's been making only his side of the bed.

☺ Life is so stressful, you've been in the bathtub since August.

☺ Your picture in his wallet has been replaced by a grocery discount card.

☺ The last night out he planned involved the laundromat.

☺ The only time he reaches for your hand is when you're reaching for your credit cards.

☺ With all your fighting, more flying objects can be seen in your house than at Roswell.

☺ You catch yourself trying to figure out a way to drop the kids off at church for summer Vacation Bible School and pick them up after the Christmas pageant.

☺ The last picnic lunch you shared was some crackers and Cheez Whiz you found under the front seat when the car broke down.

☺ His idea of spending a nice quiet evening alone involves you going somewhere.

☺ The flowers he gives you these days are seeds in a packet—and they come with a shovel.

But you *really* know it's time to go on a marriage retreat when you start getting Pearl Harbor Day and your anniversary mixed up.

In actuality, any time is a good time for a marriage retreat. It's healthy to get away for a weekend to learn more about love, marriage, and each other. And if you can't afford the expense of a retreat, just get away alone for an afternoon drive, a picnic, or a walk in the park.

You're a couple. Sometimes you have to close out the rest of the world and remind yourselves of that.

MARTHA BOLTON WAS A STAFF WRITER FOR BOB HOPE FOR OVER FIFTEEN YEARS. SHE'S THE AUTHOR OF OVER FORTY BOOKS AND IS THE "CAFETERIA LADY" FOR BRIO MAGAZINE. HER MISSION STATEMENT IS "LIFE'S TOUGH. GOD'S GOOD. AND LAUGHTER'S CALORIE-FREE!"

THE CAMPING ADVENTURE

TONYA RUIZ

P umpkin, I've got good news: We're going camping," my husband of only three months excitedly informed me.

Dread quickly overwhelmed me. "But Ron ... I've never
camped before."

"Don't worry, sugar, I'll take care of everything," he promised.

"Look," I sweetly said, "in my family, roughing it meant
sleeping at the Hilton with a window open."

We both laughed, but I was dead serious.

For weeks he shopped and packed. I had never seen him so
enthusiastic about anything. On the appointed departure date,
he was smiling as we drove off with our camping gear tied atop
our white Ford Escort. He put me in charge of reading the map.
Only three hours into our journey we were lost. "Okay," I said,
"don't get frustrated. I'm doing the best I can. Which way is east
again?

"Sugar pie," he said, "didn't you take geography in school?"

"Sure," I said, "and I got an A."

He rolled his eyes as if I'd said something impossible and
pulled the car over to the side of the road. Then he took the

map away from me, scanned it, and instantly solved the problem. "You could have followed it easier," he scolded, "if you hadn't had the map upside down."

Weary, we reached our planned camping site. "When you get away from the city lights it sure is dark," I told Ron as we looked up at the stars in the sky. "I keep hearing noises and I'm kind of afraid."

"Don't be silly, muffin, we're in the middle of nowhere. Do you think a chain saw murderer would come all the way out here?"

"Of course not," I lied.

At sunrise, he walked to the lake to do some fishing and I headed to the showers. Upon returning to our campsite, he found me in the tent crying.

"Why aren't you cleaned up, yet, honey bun?" he inquired.

"I found bats hanging from the ceiling in the shower," I sobbed.

The second night it rained and our air mattress turned into a life raft, prompting us to move to a new location the next day. On the way, Ron chose a scenic spot by a stream for our picnic. Warmed by the sun, I decided a dip in the water would refresh me.

Slowly, I began wading into the stream. Soon snakes, snakes, and more snakes gathered around me, their beady eyes watching my every move. I think I walked on water. Back on the bank, I yelled for Ron.

Upon closer inspection, he assured me, "Nothing to worry about, cookie, those are just little water snakes."

Later, we stopped the car at a different place, pulled over, and searched for somewhere to pitch our tent. Ron liked the spot. "Look, honey, we can camp here on the hill, and in the morning I can catch you breakfast from that stream."

Either I was dizzy or the ground was moving. After my eyes

adjusted, I realized amphibians blanketed the ground. "Don't worry, cupcake, those newts are just migrating," he said.

I had *had* it! I was done with all sorts of creepy creatures— and my husband's insistence that we rough it. I ran for the car and Ron followed. "I will not sleep with those things crawling all over me," I declared. "Get me a hotel room or take me home."

After finding the only lodging within a hundred miles, Ron rented a little cabin for us. *Well,* I consoled myself, *it may look slightly rustic, but at least I won't be sleeping with the newts.* Ron went out to collect kindling for the fireplace, the shack's only redeeming feature.

I decided to crawl into bed to get warm, only to find it was already occupied by dozens of tiny arachnids. Hardened by the many creatures I'd already bested on the trip, I took the pillow, brushed them away, and crawled in.

Even the bear's visit to our porch didn't scare me much. He made a lot of noise, but I knew he wanted the outdoor trash can and not me. At least the cabin had a locked door.

But around two in the morning, I heard scurrying and tip-toed over to the light. When I turned it on, mice went running in every direction. Screaming, I ran and jumped onto the bed. Ron awoke with a start and reached for his hunting rifle. "What in the world is wrong?"

"Mice," I whimpered from the middle of the bed, where I hunkered under the blanket.

"Don't worry, cream puff, they won't get on the bed," he said, before he resumed his snoring.

I shook him awake. "I thought you were Prince Charming, but I was wrong. You're Grizzly Adams." He pulled me under the covers and nuzzled me with his beard.

"I just don't get it, dumpling," he said over breakfast. "What more could you want? We've got fresh air, peace and quiet, and mountain streams full of trout!"

The adventure had invigorated him—but deflated me. "We should have discussed this in premarital counseling," I said. "I love you, but a lifetime is going to be a long time if camping is involved. Oh, and by the way, STOP CALLING ME FOODS!"

Grizzly said, "Okay, kitten, I think I have a solution."

The next morning, we drove into town and he bought me a lawn chair that he quickly dubbed, "The queen chair." He found a perfect spot next to a lake, put my chair in the sun, and placed his manly camping chair next to it.

"I am not putting that worm on the hook," I complained as he taught me how to fish. At dusk we headed back to town. Along the way I made him a promise. "I won't tell anyone that my trout were bigger than yours."

After a lovely dinner at a restaurant and hot showers at our hotel, I told Ron, "If you still want to rough it, I could open a window." We both laughed.

Our twenty-year marriage has been like that first camping trip—learning to give and take, and working together to find solutions to our problems. There have been good years and bad, but we've survived.

And last year, we found a great compromise: a beautiful cabin near a lake and across the street from a day spa. Other than a moth invasion and one mouse incident, it was an almost perfect vacation.

When you look at Tonya Ruiz, you see a pastor's wife, an active mom, a grandma, and an engaging, insightful speaker and author. To find out more: www.TonyaRuiz.com.

FIVE GROOVY WAYS TO SAY "I LOVE YOU" TO YOUR SPOUSE

PEPPER'S PIT STOPS

1. Brag on him to others, especially when he's standing next to you.

2. Read Gary Chapman's *Love Languages* together.

3. Give him a homemade "Good Attitude" booklet, featuring "good-for-one" coupons for golfing, foot massage, go-carting, computer class, or skydiving (yikes!) … whatever normally makes you roll your eyes.

4. Buy a question book, such as *The Questions Book for Marriage Intimacy* by Dennis and Barbara Rainey, or use questions from "The UnGame," and schedule twice-a-month dates to answer them. You'll be surprised how much you find out, even after twenty years!

5. Don't be ashamed of going to counseling. We all need retraining!

WHY IS IT SO HARD TO FORGIVE?

LESLIE WILSON

I've heard God's timing is perfect. So it's probably no coincidence that I read a column on the importance of apologizing on the *very* day my apology limits were stretched beyond their capacity.

Let me re-create our Monday Night Fight for you. It started when my daughter, Molly, came to me for help with her "All About Me" poster for school.

I suggested she use her All About Me poster from third grade, or even second, but her new teacher had given her a banner about the size of a postage stamp (instead of poster board), so Molly was forced to start from scratch.

Since our family had recently moved from the "Thumbing through Dust-Covered Photo Envelopes" age and into the "Digital Photography" age, Molly needed help opening photos on our computer and adjusting their sizes to fit on her poster.

My husband suggested I could do this, despite the fact that I knew absolutely nothing about digital photography. I've never even successfully used the camera. Our son's end-of-year class photos look like they were taken through a filthy lens

... underwater ... and without my contact lenses in. Now, I admit Bret hadn't spent any time with the photo software either, but at least he's familiar with the camera.

I soon learned why I had been nominated Resident Photo Expert that evening. It seems Bret had more pressing things on his mind. Reese needed to throw pitching practice. After all, he's eight, and scouts might show up at his PONY baseball games any day now.

As Dear Hubby headed outside to catch with Reese, I may have raised my voice a bit so that Molly, sitting right next to me, could hear. "I guess your Dad thinks *baseball* is more important than homework!" Bret heard ... and stormed into the office. With a thundering voice he ordered me out of the desk chair. "There's no reason for both of us to sit here and try to figure this thing out!" I noticed he was also talking in a louder-than-normal voice and accentuating certain words so I wouldn't miss his point.

Within two minutes, Bret figured out how to crop, copy, drag, reproduce, and resize photos. He even showed me how to do it. The process was indeed idiot-proof, as I proved over the next forty-five minutes.

Unfortunately, the burden to apologize was on me. I hate when that happens.

Knowing the way to a man's heart is through his stomach, I baked a fresh batch of slice-n-bake chocolate chip cookies. The look on Bret's face when he came back in the house indicated that the gesture wasn't going to be enough.

So without adding *any* emphasis to certain words, I said, "I'm sorry I raised my voice. I acted like a baby. Once I sat down at the computer and started working on the pictures, it wasn't that hard. I apologize."

Then the craziest thing happened. Contrary to popular belief, I didn't die. I even felt a little better. Especially after I had a few cookies.

Leslie Wilson, wife and mom of three, hails from Rockwall, Texas. She pens a weekly humor column, "Reality Motherhood," and speaks to thousands of moms each year through Hearts at Home, MOPS, and ECPTA. Visit www.lesliewilson.com.

FIRST CORINTHIANS 13 FOR WIVES

If I speak in the tongues of men, with all the football lingo known to man, but have not love, I am only a shrill ref's whistle.

If I cook gourmet meals that would turn Martha green with envy ... and have a dream home right out of *Better Homes & Gardens*, but have not love, I am nothing.

If I give all I possess to the poor, especially the ratty T-shirt he's had since college, but end up angering him in the process, I am nothing.

Love is patient, even when the 12,483rd sock ends up on the floor.

Love is kind, even when I've been cooped up all day and he wants to veg out.

It does not envy, even when he knows his computer screen saver's face better than mine.

It does not boast, even when I have multitasked all day long, and he can't seem to do more than one thing at once.

It is not proud when others in troubled marriages ask, "How do you do it?"

It is not rude when he asks, "So what have you done all day?"

It is not self-seeking, especially when I know I'm right!

It is not easily angered when he acts like the world revolves around him.

It keeps no records of wrongdoings, even when he says I never told him that, and I've told him ten times.

Love does not delight in evil and remind him that I told him to ask for directions, but rejoices with the truth that we reached our destination anyway.

It always protects his fragile ego, and knows when to encourage him.

It always trusts that God will take care of him, always hopes for our future, always perseveres, and never, never, ever gives up!

Love never fails.

But where there are financial problems, they will pass away ... eventually! (Please, God?)

Where there are petty arguments, they will be stilled.

Where there is talk of splitting up, it will cease.

For most of what I say is true, while some of it might be exaggerated the *teeny-tiniest* bit. But when a repentant heart cries out, forgiveness comes.

When I was a child, I talked like a child, I thought like a child, I reasoned like a child. (When I became a woman, you would *think* I would have put away those things.) Now I see a reflection of someone in the past who could love her husband only in part, because she did not completely understand love. But even though I still at times act like a child, with God's help, I'm beginning to understand love more fully.

And now these three remain: faith, hope, and love.

But the greatest of these is Love.

CRACK FILLER

DEBBIE HANNAH SKINNER

H ey, baby!!!" yelled the driver of the pickup truck whizzing by, adding a blaring staccato *Honk! Honk! Honk!* just for good measure. The greeting that would have made me laugh on any other day just aggravated me all the more as I pushed my car down the road with all my sweaty might, with my husband sitting in the driver's seat.

We had only been married a few months when this "car incident" took place. My husband had been driving alone in my 1974 sunshine yellow VW beetle, the car I'd driven since I turned sixteen, when it died in the middle of traffic on a busy street. With a *putter, putter, kaput* it lost power. Fortunately, he was able to coast to a safe side road in a residential neighborhood.

Because this happened long before the days of cell phones and pagers, he walked to a nearby business and called me to come and assist with the car. I arrived within minutes and we proceeded to search for the cause of the car problem. As I know absolutely *nothing* about cars except whether or not they are a cute color and where to insert the key and the gas nozzle, my help was limited to moral support.

Thinking the battery might be the problem, we first attempted to give the car a running "jump start" where he steered and I pushed the car backwards down the street. By releasing the clutch at just the right time, the engine was sure to start. But we tried it three times and nothing happened. I welcomed the end of this approach since: (1) it did not work and (2) it made me look like I was trying out for an episode of the world's sweatiest woman competition.

My husband then decided that perhaps all we needed to do was change the spark plugs. We drove to a nearby auto parts store, bought the correct plugs, and returned to our roadside open-air auto garage where he installed them in the Volkswagen. Unfortunately, when he turned the ignition, nothing came on but a few flashing lights on the dashboard.

"Do we need to call a tow truck?" I asked.

"No, let's try the push start one more time," he said. Thinking the car simply needed more muscle behind it, he put me behind the steering wheel and positioned himself in front of the car to apply some real brawn to the job.

That's when I saw it.

The needle on the gas gauge had settled below "E."

The problem was not the battery or the spark plugs or any number of other possible problems. The only thing that could solve our car trouble that day was a visit to the nearest filling station for a can of gas.

I howled. He came to the driver's door to see what had me laughing so hard I could barely catch my breath. When I pointed at the gas gauge and he realized what had happened, he laughed too.

My brilliant husband completed a PhD in pastoral care, and not one, but *two* master's degrees. He is handsome and fun and perceptive and loyal. He is a wonderful provider and my best friend. But that particular day, he led me to spend over two hours on a nonexistent car problem. It was one of those funny marker events in our marriage, a slice of our life together that we still laugh about.

A year later, we attended a Valentine's party for young married couples where we were one of the "couple contestants" in a version of the old TV show, *The Newlywed Game*. When asked to complete the sentence, "I knew I married a mental midget when ..." I started laughing so hard I could barely speak. I told the story of our "car incident" and guess what? The entire crowd got a big laugh out of it too. Better still, we won the game that night.

I must confess, in our twenty-two years of marriage, my husband is not the only one who has had "mental-midget moments." I've had my share as well: like the day I forgot to put my minivan in park—and watched it roll into oblivion down a hillside ravine. Or those months I tried to balance my checkbook, only to find all the deposits I *thought* I had made were really withdrawals. The list goes on.

Jesus Christ is the mortar that holds our marriage relationship together, but I think of our shared experiences, like the car incident, as being the crack filler that seals up the little crevices that creep up over time. I've discovered that the cool thing about married love, especially over the long haul, is that you get to be a firsthand, front-row witness to the silly and the sad things, to the hopes and the hurts, to the aggravations and the devastations, in someone else's life.

And they get to be there for yours.

Debbie Hannah Skinner is a "Bible teacher with a paintbrush" who lives with her husband and daughter in Amarillo, Texas. She weaves watercolors with Scripture as she ministers nationwide through Mirror Ministries. Visit www.dhskinner.com.

STARSHINE'S HOW'S YOUR INNERSTATE?

FRIENDS AT FIRST SIGHT— LAYING A FOUNDATION FOR LOVE

by Karen O'Connor

From the moment we met at a dinner party in Los Angeles, I knew I wanted to get to know this gentle man with the large blue eyes—a man who listened and talked, and laughed. He seemed like a person I could trust—a man who could be a *friend*. And he wanted to know more about me.

We didn't fall in love right away. We were friends first—good companions. We shared music and books, spent time with our children, attended church together on Sundays, and learned each other's likes and dislikes.

We also disagreed and argued. We still do sometimes. I'm spontaneous. Charles is methodical. He likes to think things through. I like to feel my way into a decision. But through it all, we've remained friends. And today, after nearly twenty years of marriage, friendship still holds us together.

As I reflect on the makeup of our friendship and our marriage, four characteristics come to mind—characteristics that have helped us dig into our pain and talk it out, as well as sit together in silence, confident of our commitment to God and to one another.

COMFORT

We've learned to ask for it—challenging as that may be sometimes—especially after we've had a hard talk, or felt alone following the death of a parent, or find ourselves stuck in regret over a past mistake or a present choice. Sometimes just a touch or a word of encouragement can make a difference. I like words, while Charles prefers touch. By learning what each other needs, we've been able to comfort one another in a way that works.

COMPASSION

We've learned about compassion the way we learned to play the piano—by practicing it! We're in this for the duration—we took our vows before God and man—so we continue to explore what it means to be compassionate. I am discovering what works: to be more sensitive than assertive, more spiritual than custodial, more nurturing than managing. And when I remember, we're both blessed.

CONNECTION

In order to nurture our connection, we've made some deliberate choices. We eat together regularly. We also play together (hiking, camping, exploring the outdoors, taking long walks). We go to the theater and to movies and to museums. And most important to us, we pray together each morning. Our faith, our family, and our friends are the strong threads that connect us to one another and to God.

CONSISTENCY

We're working on this! Being there for one another is very important to each of us. That means remaining committed to mutual respect, even when we have hard things to talk about. The challenge is to be consistent without being controlling. To us, consistency also includes being fully human—to let ourselves be known as someone the other can turn to with confidence. Even though we make mistakes, we want to be just as quick to make amends.

If someone asked us how to approach a new relationship or how to maintain one already in place, we wouldn't have to think about it. From our experience, what really counts is friendship.

Karen O'Connor is a retreat speaker, award-winning author, and writing mentor from San Diego, California. Visit Karen's Web site, www.karenoconnor.com.

OF RATS AND MEN

LAURIE BARKER COPELAND

I was minding my own business, reading quietly, when—from the corner of my eye—I saw something move. I glanced over.

Nothing.

I resumed my reading.

Scritch, scritch, scritch.

This time I kept my eyes plastered on the spot of presumed movement and waited....

To my horror, a fat, hairy rat meandered out from under my bed. *In my bedroom?* I did what any healthy female would do. I leapt up on my bed and screamed, beckoning my knight, John, to come save me.

"What's the commotion?" my husband of one month asked, galloping in atop his imaginary white stallion, his yet to be tarnished armor glinting.

"Rat!"

My stud (John, not the horse) let out a high-pitched yelp—at a decibel level I wasn't aware knights could reach—and did something akin to an Irish jig, kicking his feet into the air. Then he hopped up on the bed with me.

So much for the knight.

As we held each other like two Japanese movie victims ready to be squashed by a gargantuan creature, the rat calmly continued his quest from under the bed. At his leisure, he waddled his way to a concealed hole in our apartment's closet, stuffing falling out of his tiny little mouth.

When he resurfaced, we watched with astonishment as the rat swerved back and forth across the carpet.

Because of the wobbling, I proclaimed, "He's drunk!"

Then our four-legged visitor stopped and, in slow motion, simply teetered over onto his side. His legs stuck straight out like a taxidermic armadillo.

John offered a feeble guess: "Is he dead?" (Probably from too much alcohol consumption.)

Just when we thought it couldn't get any weirder, the "Blessed Event" happened.

The "he" was a "she," and "she" wasn't drunk, she was *pregnant!* Miniature, shriveled baby rats came popping out of the mommy rat. One, two, three (we gasped for breath), four, five (I couldn't decide if this was the coolest or the grossest thing I had ever seen in my life), six, seven little rat babies were delivered, right there in our bedroom. *Isn't that special?*

My knight, with armor slightly askew, ran around the apartment in circles debating on a method for evacuating the rat family. Finally, with his face twisted into a "this-is-so-gross" grimace, he scooped them into a shoebox—mom, kids, and all—and prepared to dump them in the woods. Opening up the lid just a tad, he said in his best mafia voice, "Get in the car, Vinnie, yer takin' a ride ..."

I gazed at my knight and realized the rats weren't the only ones takin' a ride. As we entered this life of newlywed unknowns, I brought him down from his stallion-pedestal and gave him a peck on his flustered cheek. I was beginning to discover his human side.

And I grew to love his tarnished armor even more—chinks and all.

Many of us begin our marriages with a few unrealistic expectations. Our husbands all have a certain amount of stud—or white knight—in them (at least in our eyes) before we marry.

Then the first disappointment happens. He jumps up on the bed with you instead of valiantly ridding your dwelling of a nasty four-legged invader. Perhaps he makes a poor business decision, breaks a promise, or lets his "pecs" go a little. Or maybe he does something far worse. What's a girl supposed to do when her knight's armor has a chink or two ... or three? (We won't even talk about *our* chinks.)

The pregnant rat experience was the start of a "ride" that's lasted for twenty-four years and counting. But it's so much more than just any ride: Our marriage has been like a roller coaster. It's had thrilling parts—up, up, up, when we could barely wait to find what would happen at the top—and it's had fast and furious downward plummets. It's even had unexpected, breathtaking turns.

But from a totally human standpoint, what else do we expect? When you think about marriage—really think about it—it's amazing *any* of us stay together. Marriage throws two people—who usually have opposite personalities—together. Often, they have different upbringings, social and political standards, educational values, and opinions on everything from child rearing to taste in food, décor, and music.

But for some reason, the two people still want to share their lives together. They confidently proclaim, "Our love will take us through this." *Uh-huh. Okay.* Then they throw children in the mix: adorable, turn-your-life-upside-down darlings, who will—without even trying—pit you against one another.

No wonder we want to throw our hands up in the air and wave the white flag of divorce!

But if we do that, we may miss a big part of God's plan for us. I know the struggles are a part of God's plan to make us better people, less selfish and, dare I say, more Christlike? Like diamonds in the rough.

When a diamond is first discovered, it doesn't exactly sparkle. Only after much work from machinery incessantly rubbing off all the outer dullness does one find the brilliance and natural beauty of the diamond.

My parents have been married for almost sixty years. They, too, have opposite personalities, but they've allowed a lot of their rough edges to be rubbed smooth. Although they're not perfect, their lives shine with Christ's diamond-like beauty. If *we* give up too soon, we may miss our own "buffing up" process!

On our seventh anniversary, we noticed many people were impressed with how many years we'd been married. Seven short years! Their awe grew with each passing year. When we celebrated our twentieth anniversary, our waiter asked us who had put up with more. Without hesitation, we both pointed to each other. He was taken aback and said when he asks that question, most people usually think of *themselves*.

It got me thinking. I am not exactly the best wife in the world. Far, far from it. I have done and said stupid, foolish, and selfish things. And that realization makes me appreciate John's (and God's) patience with me. Even after twenty-four years of marriage, I'm still learning. Maybe that's the secret to marriage!

STARSHINE'S SMILE MARKERS

HOLDING HANDS
by Jeannie St. John Taylor

The sight of the elderly couple shuffling down the nursing home hallway and holding hands flooded my heart with warmth. Their marriage, it seemed, was held together by a love so strong they still enjoyed holding hands in their nineties. The desire to touch hadn't dimmed after sagging muscles and wrinkles robbed them of physical beauty.

I wanted a relationship just like that. Stopping in front of them, I placed my hand on their gnarled ones. "The two of you look so sweet," I said. "I hope my husband still wants to hold my hand when we're your age."

A look of surprise flickered across the gentleman's face. Then his forehead wrinkled as he scowled and informed me, "We're only holding hands so we can stand up."

JEANNIE ST. JOHN TAYLOR, A FORMER TEACHER WITH A MASTER'S DEGREE, WORKS FULL-TIME AS AN AUTHOR AND ILLUSTRATOR. HER TITLES INCLUDE: *WHO DID IT?* (KREGEL), *AM I PRAYING?* (KREGEL), *HOW TO BE A PRAYING MOM* (HENDRICKSON PUBLISHERS), AND *101 STORIES OF ANSWERED PRAYER* (AMG PUBLISHERS).

HARLEY HONEY

BARBARA MARSHAK

As soon as my husband, John, started talking motorcycles with friends, I knew it was only a matter of time. Maybe turning forty had something to do with it. Maybe not. But throughout our ten-year marriage, I had become painfully aware of John's infatuation for all things with engines and wheels. I watched his eyes light up like sparklers every time he described the pure thrill of *hugging the road.* To prove his point, he insisted on taking me for a couple of rides.

"See!" he said, nodding, convinced I would love it just as much. "Isn't it exhilarating?"

"Don't think so," I said dryly.

"What? How can you say that?" He listened as I explained that I didn't appreciate a helmet smashing down a hairstyle I'd taken thirty minutes to fix. I also didn't like how our helmets knocked together if I leaned forward too far or the fact that shouting at the top of your lungs was the only form of communication—not to mention I didn't consider the motorcycle a family-friendly "toy." I looked him straight in the eye while reciting those reasons, but his blank smile only belied the fact that my words fell on deaf ears.

I went so far as to warn him: "If you go out and buy this *thing,* you and the guys will ride, but you won't be riding with *me.*"

John's philosophy was, "You don't really have a motorcycle unless you own a Harley," so before I could say *Live to Ride,* a shiny black Harley Davidson Road King had taken up residence in our garage. The cycle itself was just the beginning. John made countless trips to the closest Harley Davidson retailer for chrome extras, longer handlebars, louder pipes, black leather, eagle patches, boots, belts, and more black leather.

Our suburban, two-car garage suddenly became inadequate for protecting the sacred cycle and subsequent paraphernalia. John sawed and hammered into the late-night hours, and built a Harley house complete with carpet, lights, and controlled temperature—inside our garage. You can rest assured I had visions of *someone* out there snuggled up right next to it.

Now, John is the type of man who loves to have me with him whenever possible. That first summer with the cycle, he kept asking me to ride with him. I stood firm, coming up with numerous excuses as to why I couldn't.

"Guess what?" he asked one September day, his voice full of excitement.

"What?"

"Dean and Teri invited us to go on a weekend trip down along the Mississippi River. Can I tell them you'll go?" Living in southern Minnesota we have some of the most beautiful drives along the Mississippi River bluffs, and the quaint river towns dotting the roadsides are among my favorite destinations.

"Sure, that'll be fun."

Only later did it dawn on me ... *he means on the Harley!* Since it was too late to back out, I made a halfhearted attempt to find a sitter for our son and offered instead to drive our SUV and follow behind, pointing out they'd have room for extra gear that way.

For two days my son and I contentedly followed the cycles along the picturesque country byways. It was a perfect fall weekend to follow the river as it cut a blue path between the wooded bluffs hugging both sides. Several times Dean or Teri offered to drive the SUV so I could have a chance to ride on the Harley. Determined not to give in, I'd respond each time with a quick smile and, "No, thanks. I'm fine."

Finally, at one of the scenic overlooks along the majestic Mississippi, my persistent husband asked again. "C'mon ... ride with me." The look in his eyes betrayed how much he wanted me to try it, and in a weak moment I heard myself agree to a short ride.

"Just to the next stop," he promised, handing me a helmet. "It'll be great, you'll see."

Thrilled to have me join him, he cited a few brief instructions before I climbed on. The afternoon had turned sultry and hot, so I pushed up the shield on my full-face helmet in search of fresh air. After making sure I had my feet positioned correctly, he revved the pipes a few times and took off down the highway.

Try to enjoy it, I thought. *Relax. Breathe in the great outdoors. Feel the breeze.* And in the very next second a hornet flew into my helmet. The high-pitch buzzing echoed in my right ear as it proceeded to sting my cheek.

"Aaah!" I screamed while trying to sweep the nasty insect out of my helmet, only to have it sting my fingers.

Being a man of high intelligence, John realized something was amiss and immediately pulled over to the shoulder, not even *one mile* from where I'd climbed on.

"What is it?" he asked.

"There's a bee in my helmet!" I screamed, ripping it from my head.

He stared in awkward silence, not sure what to do or say as I clawed at my hair.

After assessing the sting marks on my face and hands, he took a deep breath. "Are you okay?"

I couldn't find the words.

"Would you rather get back in the truck?" he asked, ever so politely.

"No," I growled between clenched teeth. "Just—drive!" With a defiant tug, I pulled the helmet back on. John told me later that despite the nearly ninety-degree temperatures, he swore a blast of frigid air appeared out of nowhere and settled right between us.

We can look back and laugh about it now, but in truth it took us awhile to sort through our feelings about this new entity in our lives. Overall we had a strong, healthy marriage, but I wanted John to realize that as a working mom I simply couldn't drop everything and go along every time he revved up the bike. After being out of the house Monday through Friday, Saturdays were my day to do housework and spend time with our son. For me the home and family needs came first, and I didn't like it when he made me feel guilty for not going with him.

By the same token, knowing how much he loved having me tucked right behind him, I needed to recognize the importance of going occasionally ... and to make sure my attitude reflected that I *wanted* to go.

Throughout the next summer, I started riding more often as we talked through the issues and worked toward an understanding. Even though I didn't necessarily enjoy the ride itself, I liked the social interaction and friendships with other Harley couples. Through it all, I've survived freezing temperatures as well as stifling heat, bugs in my teeth, and helmet hair.

The bottom line is that at one time I was a thirty-one-year-old single mother who longed and prayed for a soul mate. God chose to honor that prayer and to him I'll be forever grateful ... even if it means being a Harley Honey.

Ride on.

Barbara Marshak is a freelance writer with numerous articles to her credit. Last summer, she attended the infamous bike rally in Sturgis, South Dakota. Barbara resides in the Twin Cities with her husband, family, and the Harley.

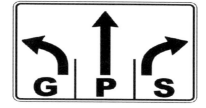

LOST? TRY GPS
(GOD'S POSITIONING SYSTEM)

For God is not unfair. He will not forget how hard you have worked for him and how you have shown your love to him by caring for other Christians, as you still do.

HEBREWS 6:10 NLT

FAVORITE OFFBEAT ROAD TRIP EXITS

Bodie, California—Bodie was one of the largest cities in the gold-digging days of California, but somewhere in the 1930s, the last person left the dwindling town. Today, it's a state park where you walk the streets, peek in the windows, and visit homes and businesses preserved just the way they were at the end of the town's heyday. As you stroll down the dusty main street, make sure you say "howdy" to the only living resident, Willy Bodie, as he stalks you from behind. Willy is a friendly black-and-white cat.

Bonneville Salt Flats, Utah—You've probably seen this place a thousand times on car commercials and didn't even know it. When the former Lake Bonneville fell below its lowest outlet centuries ago, it shrank in size and left the Bonneville Salt Flats ... miles and miles of dry, flat land. (Just perfect for a car commercial!)

We'd Lost That Lovin' Feelin'

NANCY C. ANDERSON

ADAPTED FROM *AVOIDING THE GREENER GRASS
SYNDROME: HOW TO GROW AFFAIR-PROOF HEDGES
AROUND YOUR MARRIAGE* (KREGEL PUBLICATIONS)

My husband and I met on a lovely autumn day in 1976. I was a tall, thin, twenty-year-old college girl wearing a short denim skirt and a perky Dorothy Hamill haircut. As I sat on a park bench reading a Groucho Marx autobiography, Ron walked by. He told me later he took one look at me and felt his heart dance (Ka-ching! Bling! Bling!). I was just his type: young, pretty, and, best of all, reading a book about a comedian. His first words to me were, "Is that a funny book?"

I looked up, smiled, and said, "It's great! Listen to this." Then I read him a paragraph in my best "Groucho" voice.

His face lit up. Impressed by his beautiful smile and perfect teeth, I moved over. He sat down and we talked about everything and nothing for over an hour. Then we started dating.

Before every date he made sure that he washed the car, took a shower, brushed his teeth, and put on cologne. He was always on time, greeted me with a minty-fresh kiss on the cheek, and often brought flowers. Sometimes he even brought a bouquet for my roommates. He planned our dates with military precision; he knew the who, what, when, where, and why of every event. He'd tell me if the dress code was formal or casual. If we went to a party, he'd always stay by my side, attending to my every wish.

Once, while standing in the bitter cold at an outdoor wedding, he covered me with his suit coat while he shivered in silence.

He would often surprise me with funny or sweet cards in the mail or drop a note into my purse for me to find later. One letter began, "My dearest maiden," and he signed it, "Your knight forever, Sir Ronald." Ron treated me like a princess, and I loved every minute of it!

In November of 1977, he took me back to the park bench where we met and produced a tiny blue-velvet box. Then he bent down gallantly on one knee and opened the box to reveal a sparkling diamond ring.

Ron's voice quivered as he said, "Nancy, I love you. Will you marry me?"

Tearfully, I gasped, "Absolutely!"

I envisioned our life together: seventy years full of laughter and romance in a kingdom full of love. The next month, he bought me a little starter-castle full of dreams.

Then we got married, and my Sir Lancelot became Sir-Belch-a-lot.

Overnight he became a three-ring circus of noises. While he slept, his snores rumbled and tooted like a calliope. Every morning, he blew his nose, trumpeting like an elephant. When he spit in the shower he sounded just like a tiger hacking up a hairball.

Our romantic dating rituals went out the window and selfish complacency sneaked in the back door. I was as much to blame as he. I stopped many of the behaviors that initially attracted him to me, like being flirty, funny, and cuddly. I criticized and corrected him about insignificant things, and he pulled away from me emotionally. We stopped trying to please each other and got careless with each other's feelings. He wanted more sex and less nagging; I wanted more money and less noise.

We lost our romantic spark and our sense of adventure and fun. We got off track and stopped caring about each other. I distanced myself from Ron and from the Lord, and began to believe the lie my divorced girlfriends told me: "You deserve to be happy."

I pursued my own "happiness," and went in search of greener grass. I began an affair with a married coworker. And in 1980, just before our two-year anniversary, I abandoned my husband and moved into a hotel.

But neither God, nor my husband, ever abandoned me. With the help of godly parents and the Holy Spirit, I eventually saw that true happiness, true peace, and true love could only be found if I walked in God's will. I returned home as a prodigal wife and begged for my husband's forgiveness. Mercifully, miraculously, he forgave me.

After we made the decision to reconcile and rebuild our marriage, we immediately sought advice from different sources. We went to a Christian marriage counselor, who helped us learn to communicate more effectively. We also read several books about "starting over" and attended marriage retreats and workshops. One of the most important things we did was join a wonderful church and faithfully attend worship services and adult Sunday school classes. We received solid biblical teaching from a godly pastor, and we acted on his instruction.

Our transformation was a slow process. We'd developed many destructive habits, and some of them took years to die. We decided to stay together and act lovingly toward each other, and eventually our feelings caught up with our actions. We learned that married love is not a feeling, it's a decision ... and we decided to love each other.

Since my affair twenty-five years ago, we've traveled thousands of miles, both emotionally and spiritually. Ron and I have trekked through the desert of "Hard Work" and trudged up the slopes of "Patience and Compromise." And, even though we often went swimming in Lake "I'm a Jerk—You're a Jerk," I'm thrilled to report we have finally arrived at the peaceful city of "Deeply-and-Tenderly-in-Love."

Ron and I found that the effort of maintaining a marriage is worth the rewards. My search for greener grass ended when I began to water my own lawn and love my own husband. Though it took patience, hard work, and many, many prayers, Ron and I have grown a lovely oasis in our own backyard.

We lost that lovin' feelin' but with the Lord's help, we found it again.

Nancy C. Anderson is a writer and speaker who lives in southern California with her husband of twenty-seven years and their teenage son. For more information about her books, speaking, or marriage ministry, please visit www.NancyCAnderson.com.

Starshine's How's Your InnerState?

A Kid's-Eye View of Love

"If falling in love is anything like learning to spell, I don't want to do it. It takes too long," said Leo, a seven-year-old.

Love is hard. Just ask Romeo and Juliet, or Scarlett and Rhett, or even Jennifer Lopez. What does is take to make love last? Tom (age seven) believes: "Spend most of your time loving instead of going to work." Roger (age eight) says, "Don't forget your wife's name."

Good advice, Roger!

In 1 Corinthians, the apostle Paul wrote that love is patient and kind, doesn't envy or boast, and isn't proud. It's also not rude, self-seeking, easily angered, and it keeps no record of wrongs. In other words, truly loving others requires that we put their needs in front of our own.

Some people follow the world's lead and change spouses when the current marriage gets rough. Case in point: Asked once about his impending divorce from Marla Maples, Donald Trump said, "If you have to work at it, what's the use?" (I wonder how far he would have gotten in business with that attitude!)

No, love isn't easy. But it is worth the work. Just ask any couple who has been through hard times and, with God's grace, comes out on the other side with their marriage intact.

But for those of us who will sometimes forget the apostle Paul's advice, Randy (age eight) has a suggestion: "Be a good kisser. It might make your wife forget that you never take out the trash."

PART FIVE

TIPTOE THROUGH THE TULIPS (Children's Love)

A Bad Hair Day

Ellie Lofaro

I don't know what I was thinking, but then again, that's a fairly common occurrence in my forty-fifth year on the planet. I suppose I thought it would all go smoothly ... that I wouldn't run into anyone I know ... that I could make it back in fifteen minutes. Wrong, wrong, wrong.

It didn't go smoothly at all. I ran into two people who knew me, and it took thirty-five minutes to get back into the chair at the salon where I was having my hair done. Having one's "hair done" means so many things these days. Not too long ago, it entailed a wash, a trim, and a boofing-up. Now, the "menu" is extensive and the prices are expensive. Hair is serious business and if you don't know exactly what you want, they'll happily serve you extra "portions." (Case in point: Last month, my hip, young Moroccan stylist suggested I get a few highlights to brighten my dark, one-dimensionally drab crown. I assumed she would use a medium brown, but one should never assume. It was more of a burnt orange, firey, Ragu sauce red.)

When I plunked myself into Najiba's chair that day, several weeks after the autumn-colored hair debacle, I was very clear about what I wanted to order from the menu. On that fateful day, I said, "Just a touch up for the gray roots. A good cut for the summer heat. Cover up the perpetual flame-red, please. And no highlights, thank you very much." Under protest, she acquiesced.

As usual, appointments at the bustling salon ran late. My hubby, Frank, was at work, daughter Paris was in Panama for a two-week missions trip, son Jordan was at tennis lessons, and youngest Capri was at basketball day camp. By two o'clock, I finally got invited to put a robe on. I needed to pick up Jordan by three sharp and was beginning to experience that "clock angst" only a mother can fully understand. Najiba applied color to my stubborn roots and pulled the rest of my hair straight up, a la Phyllis Diller, then sent me to the hide 'n retreat magazine section of the salon.

It began to drizzle, and Jordan called my cell phone. The poor kid was waiting under a tree and informed me lightning had struck. I kicked into Mega Mother Mode and told Najiba that I had to leave immediately and that I would be back in fifteen minutes.

A few women stared as I collected my car keys and cell phone. The receptionist smiled politely when I reached over her counter to whisper "I'll be back." As I sprinted into the rain, I glanced into the shop window in time to catch a few more looks—of disbelief, or pity, or both.

As I crossed the street toward the parking garage, I heard my name. After three consecutive *Ellies*, I turned around to meet a woman who had recently heard me speak at a luncheon. We ducked under a store awning. She acted as if I looked normal and didn't mention my hair, so I *did*. She spoke animatedly and started sharing her life story. When I apologized and explained about Jordan waiting for me under a tree, she seemed disappointed. I think she was hoping to encounter the woman she saw on the platform—but the best I could offer was a frazzled mother in a black nylon robe with hair issues. I wished her well, thanked her for her kind words, and asked her to please forget how I looked.

The rain got heavier, but I didn't mind because it brought some relief to the burning sensation on my forehead. Once in the car, I gasped at my reflection. By that point, I'd have been happy to look like Phyllis Diller. I was actually more akin to The Creepy Creature from the Black Swamp. The spikes were curling and the color was creeping toward my eyebrows. I grabbed a tissue, wiped my forehead, and exited the garage. The tennis courts were only five minutes away, but just as I was about to turn into the school, I heard a siren.

I pulled over and an officer approached. "Do you know why I pulled you over?" he asked. He glanced at my face and hair and then caught his breath. He stared as a drip of color streamed slowly down my temple and across my left cheek, halting finally at the corner of my mouth.

"For looking like The Creepy Creature from the Black Swamp?" I arched my eyebrows and cracked a half smile, testing his humor index. He had none.

"Ma'am, you were traveling thirty-four miles per hour in a twenty miles-per-hour zone."

"But Officer, this road is thirty-five miles per hour."

"Not near the school. You should know better."

"I am SO sorry! I thought that sign only applied September through June."

"Haven't you ever heard of summer school, Ma'am?" He wasn't smiling AT ALL.

"Yes Sir." I explained my predicament, informing him of Jordan's precarious position under the tree and of the imminent danger and explained further that our precious son is the only one who can carry on the Lofaro family name. I didn't mean to tear up but some color got in my eye (they don't call it chemicals for nothing!). A squirt from my water bottle brought some relief. The robo-cop stood in the rain and watched without emotion.

"License and registration please."

He told me to stay in the car. That struck my funny bone and I snickered (audibly) since I hadn't really considered getting out of the car, what with the weather and my hair and all. He obviously did not own a funny bone. By now, other mothers and babysitters were passing by, slowing down, and craning their necks to get a closer look at the Swamp Thing in the Durango. I am sure at least one woman from the PTA Board recognized me.

A full six minutes later, he returned with my license and registration.

"Okay, Mrs. Lofaro, consider this a warning. Slow down ... and ... good luck with your hair."

I thanked him profusely and sped into the school parking lot. Jordan was now waiting in a car and I beeped to announce my arrival. A tapping noise drew my eyes to the front passenger window. It was Jordan's tennis instructor (whom I had seen but not yet met) with a big smile and an even bigger umbrella. I slumped in the seat and sheepishly lowered the window. He didn't mention my hair and neither did I. He was a very kind and joyful man.

"You must be Jordan's mom! I just wanted to let you know that Jordan won a prize for being the most improved player today. He's a terrific young man."

"Thank you. Bye." I pressed the button and the tinted window made him disappear, which is what I wanted to do. Jordan jumped in the car and smirked at me during the five-minute drive back to the salon. I explained that my scalp was burning and that I did not care to discuss the matter until he was in college.

The rain stopped as I parked on the street in front of the salon and proceeded to have my hair rinsed and cut. I left the salon with a rich, deep brown tone on my hair, forehead, and ears. I also left with a lot of second thoughts: Maybe blonde dye wouldn't have damaged my skin; maybe gray hair would look more sophisticated; maybe a crew cut would be carefree.

I got home in time to microwave a jar of sauce and boil pasta. To round off the meal, I served Coca-Cola on ice and a steaming hot tube of Pillsbury rolls. My sensitive husband listened to my saga, took one look at the soggy pasta and the yeasty rolls, and insisted we go out to eat.

It all made me think: Women today are bombarded daily with messages about how we need to look, what we need to wear, who we need to be seen with, and so on. The "beauty business" makes billions, and most of us gladly contribute to that profit margin. We empty our pockets and fill our cupboards with things we "need" to make us more beautiful. All the while, we have no idea how silly we look as we strive for the world's idea of perfection.

What a relief it is to know that God has prepared a place for those of us who trust him as our Savior and Lord. What a relief to know that he loves us just as we are—chemically treated ears and all. In heaven, there will be no aging, no sagging, no striving, and no sorrows. And—please God—no hair dye.

A humorous writer and speaker, Ellie Lofaro has touched the hearts and funny bones of audiences since 1984. Ellie and her husband, Frank, reside in northern Virginia with their three children, Paris, Jordan, and Capri.

CHOCOLATE TOFFEE

Psssst! Hey, com'ere! Having a bad day? Need some chocolate?

Face it, sometimes the only two things that can make a not-so-perfect day better are prayer and chocolate. And because we Groovy Chicks share good things with each other, I'm going to let you in on my best, never-fail chocolate recipe. I would love to give credit to the recipe's original author, but all I know is that I got it from my fellow Groovy Chicks Charlotte and Rylee, who got it from who-knows-where?

I love sharing this yummy recipe with you, but if you and I ever go to the same function, you can't bring it, because this is the only thing I know how to make. Enjoy!

GROOVY CHICKS' CHOCOLATE TOFFEE:

1 sleeve of Saltine crackers
2 sticks of real butter
1 cup sugar
2 cups chocolate chips

Preheat your oven to 350 degrees. Cover a shallow pan with aluminum foil or use nonstick spray on an edged cookie sheet. Line the pan or sheet with Saltine crackers, being sure to go all the way to the edge. In a small pan, melt butter and sugar and boil for 2 minutes, stirring the mixture while it boils. Pour mixture over crackers and bake for 10 minutes. Melt chocolate chips (YUM!) in a pan or in the microwave. Take the cracker combo out of the oven and pour the melted chocolate over it. Be sure to spread it all out evenly. Finally, freeze for at least 1/2 hour and then break the concoction into pieces. Dig in!

BECOMING (ALMOST) OBSOLETE ON PURPOSE

LAURIE BARKER COPELAND

D ear Kailey,

Today you started high school. I'm trying to accept this gracefully, and I think I'm doing a pretty good job. I've figured it all out. Tomorrow morning, I'll start by putting growth-stunting pills in your Cocoa Puffs. Then I'll post signs in our front yard stating, "Enter at your own risk. Two hundred and twenty-five pound crazed father inside, looking to interview potential dates." And as you near fifteen, I plan to sabotage both of our cars, landing them at the fix-it shop—permanently.

I want to hold you close forever. Since you are our one and only, I bet I'm just a teensy-weensy bit neurotic about it. But you didn't hear that from me.

I have to face it ... I don't let go very well. That's especially true when it comes to letting go of the one my husband and I took nine years to plan for, the one I carried in my womb for almost ten months, the one I have nurtured, sacrificed for, and trained the last fourteen years. My baby, my one and only ... my Kailey.

What *is* it about this mothering thing? Since I've always

worked out of my home, I've been blessed to be able to rearrange work and volunteer at your school from the day you began kindergarten. I believe I handled that day quite well too. I waved good-bye to you on the bus then promptly got in the car and followed the bus to school ... just not too closely. But, really, I had a good reason! Your teacher had asked for my help on the first day and I was glad to assist. Over the years, I was homeroom mom, a PTA board member, and I didn't miss a performance or field trip. I patted myself on the back for my involvement. Yes, I worked out of my home, but raising you—being a mother to you, and involved in your life—was, and is, a priority.

But what is an involved mom to do now that you don't need me in the same way? Am I supposed to have an "on and off" switch between my shoulder blades so I can turn off my desire to be your always-present instructor and protector? Isn't there a class I can take on how to give you "space" so you can learn to get along without me?

Isn't there a pill I can take so this doesn't hurt so much?

And besides, here's the real kicker: I *love* being with you and your friends. You are a delight. I love your laugh, your personality, just who you are. I love it when you share your thoughts. I love it when you share with me ... you.

The irony of all this is that your dad and I deliberately waited nine years before having you, because we were such kids ourselves. I was thirty years young, and I knew that my biological clock should have been ticking. But it wasn't. We prayed that if God wanted us to have kids he'd put the desire in our hearts. Two weeks later, God changed our hearts! However, the fact remained—I was very unqualified as a potential Mother of the Year. I hadn't ever babysat; I had never even changed a diaper! I had no idea when my mothering skills would finally kick in.

Then the day came that I had you. And that's all it took. *Wham!* I was hit with the biggest gush of mother love I could ever imagine. God equipped me in a miraculous way, and I was forever changed. I no longer was a working professional just biding my time until you reached daycare age ... I was Mommy with a capital "M," gifted with a powerful love and passion for my baby. The funny thing is that all these feelings are no different from any other mom's. I was just surprised it happened to me.

But now I'm hooked. I'm so hooked I can't seem to get the hook out of my "big fish" mouth. I'm hesitant to embrace the art of letting go, but I have to trust the fact that we have "raised our child in the way you should go, and you won't depart from it" when given the opportunity. Just as God gives us a free will to choose the right or wrong way, I, at some point, have to let you go and know that his Word won't return void in your life.

We've been learning to "let go" from the day you were born. The first night home after I delivered you, your father went to the grocery store. You were in the cradle and I left you for just a moment to get something in the kitchen. When I returned, both the cat and dog had their noses in the cradle, sniffing you. Your Nana had warned me about pet saliva and the mysterious and dastardly diseases it carries to the newborn. I started to freak out. Fighting that overwhelming urge, I prayed, "This job is too big, God! I don't think I'll be able to handle it! I can't even walk away a few seconds without Dr. Germ setting in! You've got to take this panic from me. She is yours, Lord. I can't do this on my own."

God truly answered that desperate prayer, and I never freaked out like that again. (Permit me to proudly remind you that I did *not* freak out when your pacifier dropped on the floor. I let the thirty-second rule apply and didn't have to sterilize it.) Even as you grew up and had friends in a different neighborhood, I let other parents drive you. And you could stay overnight—after your father and I gave them the first and last degree and only after they coughed up their PIN and social security numbers.

The lessons in letting go didn't let up. Like when you were a year old and we visited your Uncle Bill and Aunt Lois in Connecticut. While there, your Aunt Lois covertly fed you lasagna. You never wanted to go back to strained turnips again. I don't know why. We were miffed at your Aunt Lois for introducing spicy foods before your system was ready for it. At a restaurant on the way home, we were struggling with getting you to down the Gerber food of choice when a nosy lady walked by and quipped, "Looks like Baby is ready for real foods!" She said it in a tone that called us clueless idiots. We were indignant. We were appalled at her gall. We were ... okay, maybe she was right. This was lesson number one in Letting Go.

As a young toddler, you didn't throw many tantrums. But one night was an exception. You just simply did not want to go to bed. We knew being consistent was a sign of good parenting, so we stuck to your bedtime ritual and forced you to go to bed. But there was something different about your cries that night. You were growing up. You didn't want to sleep in your 2 x 4 crib anymore. I don't know why. You were thrilled when we introduced you to your new toddler bed the next night. So maybe we *were* clueless. Left to our own devices, we would still have had you sleeping in a crib and eating mushed bananas until you were fifteen. Lesson number two in Letting Go.

But perhaps the hardest lesson was when you were in fifth grade and at a missions banquet. As we sang the song, "Lord, Send Me," you leaned back and said, "Mommy, I want to be a missionary when I grow up." I don't think you saw my tears that night as I thought, *But God, I don't want her to live in Zimbabwe!* I couldn't imagine never seeing you again, except for the occasional furlough! But once again, I painstakingly gave you to God. Lesson number three in Letting Go.

Did I say letting you go to Africa was the hardest lesson? Maybe I forgot eighth grade, when we let you have a "boyfriend," which I was assured meant hanging out at school and the occasional movie with a group of friends. I had to trust you, and you didn't let us down. Lesson number four. (And please give me credit here for not burying a tracking/video/stun gun device in your purse.)

As you continue to grow older, our similar personalities clash (who, us ... headstrong?) and I don't always like what I see. Sometimes you have an attitude problem or you carelessly forget something like your homework and I have to let you sink a little. I have to enforce rules as the Tough Mom-Cop. Stab me in the heart, why don't cha? But I have to do it. Lesson number five.

With high school will come more boyfriends, unescorted football games, learning to drive, and other "necessities" (according to you). Yes, I know those are good things ... maybe even necessary. But there is also drinking, drugs, and other temptations. These are bad ideas in which—like it or not—I have to let go and trust you will make the right choices. Will you remember the things we've taught you? Will you remember what the Bible says? When I look at you as a whole person, I appreciate the choices you make. You have a good head on your shoulders. I will have to prepare for "letting go" as you ask in the not-too-distant future to borrow the car with your newly gained license. I know there will be some more "letting go" as I trust you with the boyfriends you choose to date and the one you will someday marry.

The experts suggest parents work at becoming obsolete ... then we know we've done our job. I need to "give you space." But I also need to be "attuned and involved." So let me see if I've got this straight: I need to trust you (and God) for making the right decisions and let you learn how to get along without me.

But I also need to be there when you need me. Sounds one-sided to me!

But if I really had to admit it, I can see how it's all part of God's plan. Like the mama hen watching a baby chick peck her way out of the egg, I need to let you go. If I pecked out a nice big egg-hole for you, you would come out a weakling.

It's hard to release someone who means so much. Just ask God—he did it. But of course, he's God. And I'm just a struggling, sinful, sometimes incompetent mom who wants to do the right thing ... to let you go. One day at a time. One event at a time. One trial at a time. One decision at a time.

The question is: Do I now love you enough to let go ... once again ... and give you to God? I believe I can, because God modeled this for me. He created us, gave us our hopes and dreams, and then said, "I love you enough to let *you* go, to freely choose to love me or reject me." Because of his love for me, I am now free to fully love him in return. I guess that's what love is really all about.

Just don't talk to me about your driving. *That,* your father can handle.

STARSHINE'S SMILE MARKERS

All the art of living lies in a fine
mingling of letting go and holding on.
HAVELOCK ELLIS

A Lesson from Michael

LINDA MEHUS-BARBER

Michael had already been thrown out of two schools by the time he arrived at ours. He came to us in May, defiant and ready to prove to everyone that no one could tell him what to do.

His teacher plopped down on the staff room sofa. "That Michael's a waste of space," she spat.

I rolled my eyes, tired of her complaining. "Come on, Louise, he can't be that bad."

"Are you kidding me? That kid's a prime example of why they should make abortion retroactive. He doesn't have a chance—no dad, and his mother's a loser."

The bell rang and I stood up to leave, thankful for an end to this ugly conversation. Three steps before I hit the doorway, I heard her snarl behind me. "Well, he'll be yours in three months. Good luck!"

I shivered as I made my escape. *Some people don't belong in the classroom*, I thought.

September came. With the fresh anticipation a new school year always brings, I collected my supplies and headed to room thirteen. I always looked forward to greeting a new group of students, but this year those staff-room warnings cast a shadow of unease over my enthusiasm.

With my arms full, I entered the room. Suddenly, a whirling dervish came from nowhere. Michael bulldozed his way past the other children, sending two unsuspecting seven-year-olds smashing against the wall.

"Yeah! Teacher's here!" he yelled to the others. "Let's go!"

Darting up and down the rows, Michael skidded to a stop whenever he found a desk he liked. He'd peer inside, then wiggle onto the seat to see if it fit. He eventually chose one at the back of the fourth row, near my desk.

An hour into the day, Michael decided to entertain the class by sitting in the garbage can. Chuckling, he plunked down into it bottom-first, folding up like a "V," his scrawny legs sticking out at a 45-degree angle. The rest of the children giggled. My instinct was to ignore such attention-seeking behavior, but I couldn't. Michael was stuck.

An overwhelming desire to spout my first mini-lecture of the year came over me. "Michael," I began, but instead I bit my tongue and strode over, somehow managing to remain calm. I steadied the can between my feet and thrust one arm under his legs, the other under his armpits. As I yanked, the can broke free. Then I stumbled backward, my heel slipped on the freshly waxed linoleum, and my legs shot out from under me. In a scene that would win top prize in *America's Funniest Home Videos*, the two of us landed in a sprawled heap on the floor. The class erupted.

Later, in the middle of the math lesson, Michael popped out of his desk, stretched out in the aisle, and began a set of sit-ups. *Lord, I'm going to need patience for this child,* I thought.

That night, I knelt in my living room and prayed more fervently than usual. *Father, I'm not going to make it through this year without your help. Let me see Michael through the eyes of*

Jesus. In the silent, meditative moments that followed, I wondered yet again why I had become a teacher.

I taught at a tough school with a high staff turnover rate. Only the strongest stayed. Some moved on to schools where the children were easier to teach, while others simply burned out and ended up on long-term disability. With Michael in my class, the year was more challenging than usual, and the days dragged by. I kept a constant vigil for even the slightest sign of positive behavior to reinforce.

His reward was simple—a gentle smile, a touch on his shoulder, or a moment of eye contact with a wink, and sometimes a hug. Gradually, Michael began to blend in with the rest of the children, although he needed attention about every thirty seconds. The upcoming Christmas holidays would be a welcome relief from the constant drain on my energy and emotions. I needed a vacation—badly.

One bitterly cold day after the break, I took up my supervision post in the dark, predawn hours. The grounds were eerily empty. I trudged through the snow towards the southwest corner of the school yard, thankful for my down-filled parka and wool mittens. As I huddled in the lee of the school, I gazed across the frozen playground at the silhouetted shape of a small child stumbling through knee-deep snow, fighting the icy blast of the north wind.

Even in the semidarkness, I recognized the figure. His hands were shoved into the pockets of his tattered jacket. He hunched forward, his hood pulled up to provide at least a little protection from the cold, its fake fur trim framing his tiny face. It was Michael. *Why do kids like this never stay home from school?* I sighed.

As he drew closer, he recognized me. His little legs churned faster and he ran straight to me, causing me to teeter as he flung his arms around my waist. A pale face peered up. He had a runny nose and red, swollen eyes. Shivering uncontrollably, he groaned, "I'm so sick!"

My head dropped, and I looked down at him. "Then why didn't you stay home?" I asked, knowing a selfish motive lurked behind the question.

"I couldn't," he sniffed. His little arms reached around further, tightening his embrace. He snuggled closer. "I had to come to school—to get a hug."

I found my arms involuntarily wrap around him, pulling him firmly against my body. My chin rested on the top of his head. A tear escaped and instantly froze to my cheek, but on that bitterly cold morning, a new kind of love entered my heart—Jesus' love for this little boy.

I've often thought about Michael. I don't know what happened to him after he left our school, but I do know that my understanding of love changed dramatically because of him. Over the years, as other children like Michael appeared at my classroom door, I took what he had taught me about love and gave each of them a reason to get out of bed and come to school. Daily I would pray, *Father, let me see these children through the eyes of Jesus.* The answer to that desperate plea softened my heart so that I was able to love even the most unlovable.

I taught for ten years at that school. During my last year, a tough and hardened little girl came to me with the label, "behavior disordered," a label she had earned by biting, kicking, and scratching her previous teachers. In June, as I packed to move on, a tearful Jamie crept to my side and shoved a crumpled piece of paper into my hand. I smiled, then unfolded it and smoothed out the wrinkles. "Why do you have to go?" she had scrawled. "I'll miss you. Thank you for teaching me to love."

As I knelt down, my arms reached out, wrapping around her shoulders and pulling her close. The lesson from Michael had touched another heart.

Linda Mehus-Barber lives in Crescent Beach in Surrey, British Columbia. She currently teaches at Regent Christian Academy. Linda loves to hike in the mountains or walk along the beach with her husband and dogs.

STARSHINE'S HOW'S YOUR INNERSTATE?

JUST LOVE THEM

During the past year, someone I dearly love has been going through a trial—and I have felt utterly helpless. I have prayed with and for my loved one, and I've shed buckets of tears and said (what feels like) thousands of prayers. I've asked for others to pray, and I've claimed Scripture promises. But still, the problem has persisted. One night, I cried out to God, and tried (!) to listen to what he would have me do. And you know what I heard him whisper? *Love them.*

I thought I heard wrong. "LOVE? That's it?!" I questioned.

My goal-oriented, fix-it personality tried to argue with the maker of the universe—like that's ever smart. "God," I pleaded, "couldn't I make a phone call, start another prayer chain, listen to a sermon and pass it on, or something along those lines?"

No, he distinctly said, *I just want you to love them.*

So I loved the person, as much as I knew how. And the problem didn't go away—but my anxiety did.

Funny how that works.

LADYBUG LETDOWN

ANDREA CHEVALIER

Snips and snails and puppy-dog tails ... according to the rhyme, that's what little boys are made of. Girls, however, are made of sugar and spice and everything nice. So you can imagine my surprise when my sweet, sugary, and spice-coated daughter became fascinated and fell in love with bugs. To be specific, her insect of choice was the ladybug. At least that's sort of feminine, right?

Audrey and her friend, Gracen, loved the creatures. They had ladybug clothes, ladybug necklaces, and even ladybug bracelets. As a matter of fact, when I told the girls we could raise ladybugs for part of our homeschool co-op's unit on insects, their response was, "Hip, hip, Hooray!"

Since I volunteered to order the ladybug larvae and transfer them to their little house so they could be left safely in our classroom for all the kids to enjoy, Audrey's impatience surfaced the day after she watched me fill out the order form. She kept asking questions like:

"Are they here yet?"

"When are they going to get here?"

"Do you think they forgot about us, Mom?"

"Maybe we should check the mailbox!"

I heard those kinds of comments several times a day. Though I tried to explain that it would take a couple of weeks for the ladybugs to be delivered, her five-year-old mind couldn't quite grasp how long those two weeks were. And though she thought it took "forever," the big day finally came.

Audrey was fascinated as she watched me put the ladybug abode together. She couldn't stop touching it. But when I took the ladybug larvae out of the box, a huge look of disappointment washed over Audrey's face. She had expected fully grown ladybugs, not these "baby ladybugs." With sorrow in her eyes and voice, she looked at me and said, "You lied to me. Those are not ladybugs! They're just plain bugs!"

My heart nearly broke. I had ordered the ladybugs out of my love for her, since I knew how much she would enjoy raising them. I wanted to watch her face as she observed God's fascinating plan for nature being played out in front of her day by day. However, she didn't anticipate that future blessing—or the love behind my gift.

Then a voice spoke to my heart, and it was so audible I nearly believed it came from a person in the room. *I understand your hurt. I sometimes feel that way, too.*

I suddenly realized that I tend to respond to God the same way Audrey responded to me: with disappointment, sorrow, and distrust. God loves me and has my best interests at heart, but he also sees "the big picture." When he hears my prayers, he sees the end result of any answered requests and knows exactly what I need. However, when his gifts do not meet my expectations, I am quick to complain instead of expecting the best from him.

With a repentant heart, I apologized.

I finally convinced Audrey just to trust me and wait. Over the next few weeks she watched the bugs closely and kept a journal of her observations, but she continued to stay skeptical until the day the first adult ladybug emerged from its chrysalis.

When it happened, she warmed my heart with the sweetest smile as she said, "You were right, Mommy. They were ladybugs after all."

I had such pride and love in my heart as I watched Audrey learn to trust. I pray I will always turn to my Father, who definitely knows best, and express the same confidence in his wisdom when my own "larvae" transform before my eyes into beautiful gifts.

Andrea Chevalier is the founder of Abundant Living Ministries, through which she inspires women to live life daily through Jesus' joy and strength. She lives in Waxahachie, Texas, with her husband and two daughters. Visit www.andreachevalier.com.

FIVE GROOVY WAYS TO SAY "I LOVE YOU" TO YOUR KIDS

PEPPER'S PIT STOPS

1. Make scrapbook pages for each year of their life. Jot down your thoughts and feelings about momentous occasions (e.g., the day they were born, potty training, coming of age, the day they graduated, or when they finally succeeded in an area you've worked on together).

2. Get to know their friends. Carting a vanload of kids around is a great way to learn more about your child's friends!

3. Discover their learning style and base your communication on that knowledge. Great resources: Marlene LeFever's book, *Learning Styles: Reaching Everyone God Gave You to Teach,* or Cynthia Ulrich Tobias's book, *The Way They Learn.*

4. Volunteer in their school or for other activities. Being involved sends the message that they are important to you.

5. Talk with them and ask questions. Let them know how special they are. (Be sure and give *specific* examples of why you are proud of them.)

JUST AN ORDINARY ROCK

TAMA WESTMAN

On a road trip to visit the grandparents in Atlanta, I took a detour to the Biltmore House in North Carolina. A Southern belle at heart, I had always wanted to visit the Vanderbilts' homegrown castle. The Biltmore is a slice of life from our American version of royalty. Quickly deciding that the children were old enough (at three and four) to know their manners and not touch the breakables, I exited the Blue Ridge Parkway and followed the signs.

The kids behaved wonderfully and we talked together about what it would be like to live in a house with maids and butlers and be able to look out at mountains every morning. We lived in Memphis, where the landscape is as flat as an ironing board. It took nearly two hours to walk through all the public rooms at the Biltmore; afterwards, our legs ached and our tummies groaned for food.

Unable to pay the lofty prices of the on-site restaurant, we picnicked with sack lunches under the shade of a magnificent oak on the grounds and watched the red-tailed squirrels chase each other.

"Momma," asked my three-year-old, "wouldn't you like to live here some day?"

Devin is my little dreamer.

"I'd love to live here!" I said, catching his fun spirit. "We'd have grand parties and horses in the stables."

"And flowers in every room," piped Shana.

"And dogs?" Devin asked.

"And lots of dogs." What Devin wanted most in life was a dog, a four-legged brother who would run about and be his best friend. In those years, we lived in a town house, and pets were not allowed.

"One day, when I grow up, I'm gonna buy this place and then you can come live here with me."

I half believed him. If anyone could buy this place, it would be Devin.

We finished our peanut butter sandwiches and enjoyed the rest of the beautiful summer day.

Months later, my husband surprised me after dinner with a cake and a bouquet of flowers to celebrate our anniversary. The children made cards with construction paper and crayons. Shana, my quiet four-year-old, gave me one of her necklaces, a thin gold chain with a heart hanging from it. "That's because hearts mean love and that's what an an'vers'ry is."

My own heart ready to burst, I hugged her tightly. Then Devin stepped close to my chair, his right hand squeezed tight inside his left. Whatever he was holding, I knew it meant a lot to him. He slurped a quick kiss across my cheek and put his treasure in my hand.

It was just an ordinary rock.

Trying to be a good mom, I thanked and hugged him too, but when I turned to speak to my husband, Devin interrupted, "Momma, didn't you get it?"

"Yes, honey, I got it. I got the rock."

"No! It's not just any old rock," he said, disgusted with how dense I could be. "I've been saving it for you. I took it from the driveway at the Biltmore House. You can keep it till we move there, and then you can put it back."

I don't think I stopped crying for a week. In fact, to this day I get teary-eyed over that little pebble. It still sits, nearly twenty years later, on the table next to my favorite chair. Whenever I touch that precious stone, I mentally run a finger down my son's cheek. It belongs near my chair. It belongs near my heart.

Many of life's most precious gifts come at no cost: the bold crocus that creeps up through the snow when winter still swirls; the mockingbird's operetta in the early morning hours; the fresh, blossom-laden breeze that wafts through the air from the lilacs in spring.

The greatest gift of all is God's presence in our lives each day. And not just his presence, but his presents. How blessed I am by a God who shows me his love through the gifts of a loving home and a child's gift snatched for a dream.

Just an ordinary rock, indeed.

Tama Westman writes from her home in beautiful Minnesota. She has been married to the love of her life for twenty-four years and has two adult children. To read more, please visit www.tamawestman.com.

FAVORITE OFFBEAT ROAD TRIP EXITS

The Keys, Marathon, Florida. If you stay overnight in a hotel, you can walk out one door to see the sunrise and the opposite door to see the sunset! Interacting with the adorable dolphins in Key Largo, Islamorada, or Marathon is a bonus.

Thousand Islands, New York. Not just a salad dressing! More than seventeen hundred islands (some no bigger than rock tips, some only big enough to house a summer home or two) dot the St. Lawrence River, making the region swell with beauty.

FOR THE LOVE OF BOYS

CARON CHANDLER LOVELESS

EXCERPT FROM *HONEY THEY SHRUNK MY HORMONES*

(HOWARD PUBLISHING)

A son is a son till he takes a wife,
but a daughter's a daughter all of her life.

—Unknown

B ased on the way things are heading at my house, all I can say is: If you've been blessed with a daughter, give thanks! Even if you don't care for the guy she's dating or the way she colors her hair, even if (for the moment) you are not on the best of terms, the fact that you have a daughter is significant cause for rejoicing. Why? Because stats from as far back as the Stone Age show that most of the world's daughters live closer to, keep in better contact with, and pay more attention to their moms than sons do.

Not that I, the mother of zero daughters, am jealous. But sometime, when God has a minute, I would like to ask what he had in mind when he shuffled the deck of humanity and dealt my sisters three queens each while slipping me three jacks.

Before my family reached its current stage, I felt blissfully happy with my lot. Believe me, I love my boys. But the older they get, the more I notice a discrepancy between the sexes.

The Glory of Girls

I have noticed that a daughter has a way of remembering her mom's favorite color. She remembers her mom's ring size, shoe size, and blouse size (which she knows is not the same as her mom's pants size, but she'll never tell). A daughter is good about calling to find out things (like what the doctor said or how the diet's going) or to pass on the recipe for Whipped Tofu Fondue she saw on morning TV. She knows the movies her mom has seen and the books her mom has read, and she asks about them. A daughter even knows the day, month, and year her mother was born.

Now your average son (Lord bless him), if asked to recount just one of the above items about you, would likely keel over from a brain freeze. But let GuyTalkRadio throw out a trivia question like, "On lap ninety-one of the Daytona 500, what driver was disqualified for unsportsmanlike conduct the same year Emmitt Smith ran for more yards than the combined scores of all the NHL hockey teams in 1977, 1987, and 1997?" and you know full well he would be the first caller to blurt out to all of Radio Land, "Richard Petty's crazy cousin, Hank."

Meanwhile, not only does your average daughter have all your preferences catalogued (in alphabetical order, no less), but—especially after she moves out—she wants to do things with you, such as meeting for lunch at Aunt Pitty Pat's Porch or Victoria's Tea Room and Gardens. In fact, the lunch is likely to be her idea, and she may even bring some kind of gift—maybe a sterling silver pie server, because when she saw it, it reminded her of the times the two of you baked pies together when she was little. Of course this remembrance makes you all watery-eyed, which automatically sets off a similar reaction in her, and something female within her causes her to reach over and squeeze your arm. And for a second or two you both sit there, all aglow.

Now, your average son would not come within ten football fields of Aunt Pitty Pat's. This is because most boys are born with a-*china*-phobia, which seriously hampers their ability to withstand chitchat, eat from Wedgwood plates, or sit for long periods of time in miniature chairs with claws where there should be feet.

BOYS KNOW THEIR DISASTERS

The news about boys is not entirely grim, however. Sons—especially grown ones—are great to have around in the event of an emergency or natural disaster. (Daughters are little help in these cases, unless you can find some practical use for unbridled hysteria.) A son really shines when, for example, you raise the blinds one morning and happen to see that a sinkhole the size of a semitruck has opened up in your backyard. Or when Storm Tracker 9 reports that a Category One hurricane has been spotted two thousand miles off the coast of Africa and you need someone to tape up the windows.

Such situations call for decisive action—which your average son can solidly handle, because he's spent his childhood watching *Super Friends*. From this and other television shows, a son knows to search the perimeter for suspicious signs of intrusion if you hear a strange noise, and when he is satisfied that you, his mother, are safe, he will then take it upon himself—without being asked—to fully inspect the contents of your refrigerator (but only as a precaution).

Your average daughter may not know what to do with a disaster, but she is your kindred spirit. She will sit with you and watch the whole *Anne of Green Gables* trilogy without making a single wisecrack. The innate "homing device" she was born with keeps her heart always tracking *mom*ward, even when she gets married and moves to Alabama.

That reminds me of one of the most famous verses in the Bible, Genesis 2:24, which says, "For this reason a man will leave his father and mother and be united to his wife." Notice it does not say, "For this reason a *woman* will leave her father and mother." Wonder why?!

No Mistake about the Joy They Make

By now I suppose there's a slight chance you have mistakenly assumed that I might be ungrateful for the three highly intelligent, immensely creative, ruggedly handsome young men I have had the privilege of bringing into this world at a measly sacrifice to my C-sectioned, stretch-marked, spider-veined body—those same boys I breastfed, potty-trained, home-schooled, and cooked, sewed, and vacuumed for. The ones I prayed for, planned parties for, wrestled with, and cried over.

The fun-loving fellows with whom I played patty-cake, peek-a-boo, trucks, monsters, I spy, dress up, hide-and-go-seek, capture the flag, Simon says, red light/green light, Twister, Monopoly, football, baseball, basketball, tennis, bowling, billiards, race cars, skateboard, checkers, cards, and air hockey.

The young men I worked night and day to support, encourage, pep talk, praise, yell at, and stomp, clap, and cheer my guts out for.

The unforgettable guys I strolled, bicycled, wagon-rode, grocery carted, merry-go-rounded, swung, burped, cherished, spoiled, pampered, took zillions of pictures of, videotaped, and carted in my body, under my heart, on my back, on my hip, and in my arms.

The precious, priceless boys I kissed and patted and bear-hugged and squeezed and tickled and snuggled and stroked more times per day than the law allows.

Those special ones I tucked in, woke up, bathed, rocked, sang to, smiled at, longed for, and never, ever got tired of staring at or being with.

If previously I gave you the impression that I am in any way sorry for the more than twenty-five years I have invested my body, soul, mind, and spirit into those boys—oh, no. It's the opposite. They have been my highest joy.

Taking One for the Team

The tough part, the part I'm wrestling with just now, is that they are just about grown and gone now, and this is one mom who has never been anything but a player. It's hard being told to sit on the bench now. It's hard to hear, "You stay here while we go play somewhere else." I love being part of my sons' lives. I adore my boys. They make me laugh—and keep me young. Besides, why break up a good team?

I know. This is the way families go. But I don't much like it.

Of course I will get to see them from time to time. And every now and then they just might let me back in the game to bunt or pinch-hit. Maybe. We'll have to see. You know how boys are.

Caron Chandler Loveless is a speaker and best-selling author of Hugs from Heaven: Embraced by the Savior *(Howard Publishing);* The Words That Inspired the Dreams *(Howard Publishing); and* Honey They Shrunk My Hormones *(an Angel Award winner). She lives in Orlando, Florida. Contact her at www.caronloveless.com.*

Lost? Try GPS
(God's Positioning System)

But I lavish my love on those who love me and obey my
commands, even for a thousand generations.

Exodus 20:6 NLT

Why?

S H A N N O N   W O O D W A R D

Why did you pick this store, Mom?"

I sighed. Zac had finally done it. He had completely and utterly drained me. After a whole day of "Why this?" and "Why that?" I had reached my limit. Apparently that 238th question pushed my tilt button.

"No more 'why' questions tonight, Zac."

"Why?"

"Just because. You don't really want to see my head burst, do you?"

"Why would it do that?"

"No more!"

For nine blissful seconds, silence filled the car. Then ...

"Why are you parking here?"

Why, indeed.

Years ago, as a new mother with a clean slate, I vowed a few things. I vowed to be approachable, understanding, and fun-loving. I've tried hard over the years to keep those promises. But in those early days of motherhood I also promised myself a whole list of "nevers," which I found to be much harder to keep. I vowed never to lose my temper. I vowed never to make a big deal over bunched-up socks and inside-out shirts. And I compiled a long list of banned phrases which I vowed never to utter in the presence of my son, phrases such as:

Do I *look* like the maid?

How many times do I have to tell you ...?

Do you *want* a spanking?!!

Your room looks like animals have been living in it.

Because I'm the mother.

I cannot tell a lie. I've said every one of those phrases at least once in the course of my mom career. Some, I've said twice. But despite failing miserably with those first four phrases, I felt confident I would never, ever, *ever* utter the fifth. "Because I'm the mother" seemed like a cop-out to me. How desperate must one become to stoop to something so juvenile? And what could possibly be so hard about just explaining your reasons to your child?

From the get-go I was an idealist. I pictured myself as the kind of mother who would stop whatever I was doing, kneel down eye-level with my adorable child, and gently lead him to an understanding of why I had made whatever decision I had made. I envisioned Zac beaming at me as he said something like, "Thank you, patient and marvelous mother. Now I understand."

Oh—and in these visions my hair was shampoo-commercial perfect and I wore a flowing white dress with nary a stain, spot, or wrinkle. And we were in a park.

For a time, I was that kind of mother (minus the hair and dress). No matter what Zac asked, I gave him a full explanation. But the tone of his questions differed back then, making it easy for me to hold on to my idealism. When he was young, his "why" questions were simple. When he asked why a rock sunk when he threw it in the pond, I patiently explained gravity. When he asked why the moon followed him, I introduced him to the solar system. I saw those moments as teaching opportunities.

Then, around the time of Zac's seventh birthday, something unexpected happened. It occurred exactly *on* his birthday, if memory serves me correctly—at the stroke of midnight. I didn't hear it; I think only Zac and the neighborhood dogs caught the sound, but from somewhere distant, an alarm sounded, signaling the start of stage two in his development. Overnight, Zac's "why" questions took an unsettling turn. Suddenly, his interest shifted from getting answers to challenging my every move. All my motives became suspect. If I announced that dinner would be at 6:00, he wondered aloud what was wrong with eating at 5:00. If I bought orange juice, he'd question whether apple juice would have been a smarter choice.

These days, all his questions have a bare-light-bulb-dangling-over-a-hard-wooden-chair tone. To my ears, "Why did you buy this instead of that?" sounds for all the world like, "Where were you on the night of June third?"

That's only about 98 percent of the time, however. The other two percent of the time, his questions are heartwarming, innocent, and completely devoid of malice:

"Why did Jesus let all those people hurt him?"

"Why do we say '12:00' when it's really 11:60?"

Or my favorite, "Why do you love me, Mom?"

I could answer those types of questions all day long. But alas, as Zac wrestles for a little autonomy, he sees me less and less as his all-knowing dispenser of wisdom. I'm no longer his personal encyclopedia, and I miss that role.

I'm sure it's just a phase. I have every confidence this will pass and he'll return to the compliant, accepting, trusting child he once was. Or ... will he? Because if I'm honest—really and completely honest—I have to admit that *I'm* not always a compliant, accepting, trusting child. In many ways, I'm not that different from my son.

I've definitely asked my share of questions:

"Lord, why is it taking so long for you to change me?" This implies he's slow. It says nothing of my disobedience or resistance to sanctification.

"Lord, why won't you let us have ten children?" This questions his sovereignty and his wisdom. Maybe I'd ruin ten children. Maybe he knows that.

"Lord, why don't you just *make* me lose those twenty pounds?" This implies that because he's bigger, stronger, and all-powerful, he should step in and clean up my overwhelming and discouraging messes. What it says about me is ... well ... enough about me.

Although I know God's patience is infinitely greater than mine, I have to wonder if he ever tires of my endless stream of questions. I wonder if he has a limit, and if so, what happens when it's reached?

I reached my limit (temporarily) when the tone of Zac's questions changed. At that point, after seven years of corralling that most-dreaded phrase, I found it popping out of my mouth left and right, seemingly of its own accord.

He'd frown as I dished up dinner. "Why can't you just make a grilled cheese sandwich for me and then you and Dad can eat meatloaf by yourself?"

"Because I'm the mother."

"But why ... 'Because I'm the mother'?"

I found I liked those powerful words. Not that Zac ever really heard the wisdom *behind* them. He didn't know they meant "I'm older, bigger, stronger, and wiser. Trust me. I know what's best." He didn't get all that, but he never did figure out how to respond, either.

"Because I'm the mother" was about all I said for the first

two months after discovering how delightful it felt. Eventually I had to harness myself and reserve that sentence for the really desperate moments.

In his own way, God says those same words to us. When Job asked for an answer to his suffering, a reason for the trials he had endured, God responded with a perfectly God-like answer. Rather than justify his purposes or explain his holy plan, he simply reminded Job of his wisdom and power. *Where were you when I laid the earth's foundation ... marked off its dimensions ... shut up the sea behind doors ... made the clouds its garment? ... Will the one who contends with the Almighty correct him?*

Translation: "Because I'm God."

Job's answer was rightfully humble. *Surely I spoke of things I did not understand, things too wonderful for me to know.*

Translation: "I'm not God. I'll try to remember that."

God wants us to trust him instead of constantly questioning his ways. He says that quite clearly in Psalm 46:10: *Be still, and know that I am God.*

One afternoon, after a full day of answering questions and defending myself, I finally said to Zac, "You know what? When I say no to something, instead of questioning me, it would be nice if you just said, 'Yes, Ma'am.'"

Zac was quiet for a moment. Finally he nodded. "I bet that would be a nice treat for you, huh, Mom?"

Maybe God would like a nice treat once in a while. Maybe he'd like me to express my absolute trust in his wisdom, his sovereignty, and his love. Maybe he'd like me to just say, "Yes, Sir" once in a while.

I'll try not to question so much. Except I do need to ask this one last, nagging question. I just have to know.

Lord, why do you love me?

Shannon Woodward is a Calvary Chapel pastor's wife, mother of two, and author of two books, including Inconceivable: A Journey to Peace after Infertility *(Cook Communications). For more info, visit her ministry Web site, www.shannonwoodward.com, or blog, www.windscraps.blogspot.com.*

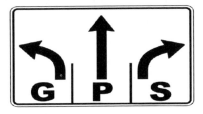

LOST? TRY GPS
(GOD'S POSITIONING SYSTEM)

How great is the love the Father has lavished on us, that we should be called children of God!

1 JOHN 3:1

PART SIX

Nowhere to Run, Nowhere to Hide
(God's Love)

BOILING POTATOES

KITTY CHAPPELL

It happened without warning. From the corner of my eye, I saw Jerry turn and look at me. As he sat there gazing, the lights from the movie screen flickered across his face, and my heart sank. I recognized that look. Jerry had just been hit by Cupid's love-tipped arrow.

Oh, no! I thought. *I never should have started dating him.*

I rarely dated non-Christians. I believed God's admonition in 2 Corinthians regarding marriage: "Do not be yoked together with unbelievers.... What does a believer have in common with an unbeliever?" To marry a nonbeliever would be like trying to mix oil and water. Besides, how could I ask the Holy Spirit to work in the heart of my husband if that heart didn't belong to God?

As director of our small church choir, I was often introduced to young men dragged to church by their mothers in hopes that they might be attracted to the blonde choir director—and maybe take a more serious look at their spiritual needs. Mrs. Chappell was no exception. After introducing her son Jerry to me one Mother's Day, we started dating.

Neither Jerry nor I wanted a serious relationship. My dream was to go to college and he wanted to start his own business. And we both knew I would never marry a man who wasn't a Christian, which he wasn't. So we relaxed and had a wonderful time together. He taught me to bowl. We enjoyed church outings, beach parties, grunion hunting, and miniature golf. And he came to church—regularly. Everything was great until Cupid hit him that night.

Well, what should I do now? I wondered. I really enjoyed his company, but I knew it wasn't fair to continue dating him. A week later, I gently explained the spiritual wisdom of our parting to Jerry. He wasn't happy, but he understood and accepted the news graciously. I spent the next long weeks missing him but determined to stick to my decision.

One evening my phone rang. It was Jerry. *I hope he's not calling to try and get together again.* After light chitchat, Jerry paused, then asked, "How do you boil potatoes?"

Following his discharge from the Marines, Jerry had moved back home with his parents where he paid them for rent and food. But his folks were out of town and he had to fend for himself in the kitchen. After instructing him in this simple procedure, I sensed he had more on his mind.

Finally, he stammered, "I need to talk with you about something."

Suspecting the "something" involved me, I braced myself, planning my response. I was unprepared for his next statement.

"I want to become a Christian."

Trying to get at the truth without sounding harsh, I said, "That's strange. You've been attending church constantly for months since we first met and now, all of a sudden—after we've broken up—you're interested in becoming a Christian?"

Jerry fell silent. *Did I offend him by my honesty?* I wondered.

"It's true. I don't want to stop seeing you," he admitted. "But this is much more important. This is an issue I must address, even if we never date again. This is about my eternity, not my love life." I sensed the urgency in his voice. "But I need help."

"Just pray, ask forgiveness, and invite the Lord to come into your life and he will," I replied, trying to shake off my suspicion. "You know all the Scriptures as well as I do. You don't need me or anyone else to help you become a Christian."

"I know," he said, "but ..."

My heart softened. "Would you like to meet me at church? I have a key. We can pray together."

"Yes," he said gratefully.

We walked the aisle to the front of the sanctuary and sat in the first row. Jerry sat stiffly, forehead furrowed, fingers drumming silently on his armrest.

"What are you thinking right now?" I asked gently.

"I'm worried—and afraid."

"Why?"

"I know I need Christ and I want him in my life because of this emptiness," he said, touching his chest. "After we broke up I thought I felt empty just because I missed you. Then I remembered everything I'd learned these past months—how we are born with a God-shaped vacuum that only God can fill, that we can reach him only through Christ, and how Christ loved us and gave his life for us." He continued, "I know if I don't accept Christ I'll be separated from God and all that is good for eternity, and I'd still be empty."

He looked at me and grinned.

My heart quickened. *What's happening to me?* I asked myself, puzzled.

"Even though you're an adorable blonde, I don't think even you could fill this emptiness," he said. "Only God can do that. So what do we do next?"

"That's up to you. All you need to do now is pray."

"I don't know how," he stammered.

"Just talk to God like you're talking to me. Be honest. Ask him to forgive your sins. Tell him you want to give your life to him."

Unclasping his hands, Jerry slowly bent forward. Looking at me sideways, he said, "That's the part that bothers me."

"Which part?"

"The part about giving my life to Christ."

"I thought that's what you wanted," I replied.

"I do. But I'm afraid if I give my life to Christ, I will never have any more fun."

I squelched a desire to laugh. "Why on earth do you think you'll never have any fun as a Christian?"

"Well," he explained, "some of the best times in my life were when I drank with my buddies. We let our hair down. In the Marines we guys always drank—and usually got drunk. Later we'd sit around and relive our escapades and have a good laugh." He added, honestly, "Though I rarely drink now, I like those memories and would miss being able to do that."

Lord, what do I say now? I prayed. *Drinking or not drinking isn't what's at stake here. I know your salvation has nothing to do with good or bad habits, but Jerry doesn't—this is an important issue with him. I need help, Lord!*

Flipping through my Bible, I read: "Therefore if any man be in Christ, he is a new creature: old things are passed away; behold, all things are become new" (2 Corinthians 5:17 KJV).

Out loud, I said, "Jerry, when we become new creatures we develop new desires. Don't worry about what you might give up, think about what you'll gain. Life is often about letting go of old things to make room for the new."

He stared at me intently. *Don't get distracted by those blue eyes*, I cautioned myself.

"For example," I continued, "when you get married, you'll have to give up your old girlfriends."

"What!" he exclaimed, in mock horror.

Ignoring him, I continued. "When a man marries, he starts a new and exciting life that includes a wife—one whom he loves enough to make a lifelong commitment. He *wants* to give up his single lifestyle and develop new desires to do things that will please his wife and not just himself. He'll cultivate new habits by including her in all his decision-making, when before he just did what *he* wanted."

Jerry nodded in understanding.

"However," I continued, "if on his wedding day he obsesses about all the things he'll be expected to give up, then he'd better not get married. He's not ready."

I placed my Bible on the pew between us. "That's how it is with a commitment to Christ. You better want him in your life so much that you are ready to put him first, regardless of what he might expect of you."

"I understand," said Jerry. "I really am ready." He flashed that irresistible smile, "I was just having premarital jitters."

"Are you ready to take the plunge now that we're through with your spiritual premarital counseling?" I asked, also grinning.

"Yes, but I want to kneel."

We knelt side by side in the quietness. A strange stillness filled the room, as though all of heaven held its breath.

"God, I really do want you in my life. I'm sorry for all my sins. I do want to become a new person in you. Help me to trust you and not be afraid of the future. Please take away this emptiness that I've been trying to fill with earthly things and fill me with your love ..."

In the stillness, he continued to pray—and pray, and pray. He shifted positions and struggled for new words.

"Jerry," I whispered, "what's wrong?"

"I don't know," he whispered back.

"Let's talk for a minute."

We arose and sat again in the pews. I took his hand. His blue eyes were clouded with confusion.

"I don't understand—I prayed and nothing happened."

"What did you expect to happen?"

"I expected to become a Christian."

"What makes you think you didn't?"

"Because I didn't feel anything—aren't you supposed to *feel* something?"

"Were you sincere when you asked God to forgive your sins and come into your life?

"Yes."

"Do you believe the Scripture that says, 'Everyone who calls on the name of the Lord will be saved'? And the one that says, 'Though your sins are like scarlet, they shall be as white as snow'?"

"Yes."

"And the verse that says, 'If we confess our sins, he is faithful and just and will forgive us our sins and purify us from all unrighteousness'?"

"Of course, I do. Why?"

"Because if you do, then you *are* a Christian. Is God a liar?"

"No, of course not."

"Well, since he said he'd do all these things when a person comes to him in sincerity, and since you say that you were sincere when you prayed to him, and neither you nor God is lying, then you *must* be a Christian."

His face suddenly relaxed. "That's right," he said, beaming. "I guess I am. But why don't I feel anything?"

"Spiritual rebirth is a unique personal experience. Each of us has our own personality, so not all spiritual experiences are the same. Some people feel bolts of joy and exhilaration and some feel an immediate lifting of burdens and a strong assurance that they now belong to God. That's how I felt. Others feel nothing at the time, but later experience an affirmation of their decision. In some way, and in his time, God will reveal to you that your experience is real. Just trust him to keep his promises.

"And," I added, "don't go listening to the devil when he comes lurking around telling you that nothing really happened. He wants you to think you just imagined it and that you're a fool for even thinking such things, but he's a liar."

"Okay," he promised.

"Scripture tells us the angels rejoice when someone becomes a Christian. Since they are rejoicing now, why don't we? Let's go for a Coke!"

Jerry eagerly agreed.

After church the following Sunday, Jerry whispered, "It happened! Last night I suddenly had this feeling—like love being poured all over me—and my heart filled with unbelievable peace! You were right. God gave me a feeling that validated my experience—in his time. Thank you, for all of your help."

I gave Jerry a long hug, and whispered my gratitude to God. At that moment, however, only God knew that I had just hugged my future husband—a husband of forty-seven years. And one who, all those years later, still wouldn't know how to boil potatoes.

Kitty Chappell, a luncheon and retreat speaker and author, lives near Phoenix. For information about her book, Sins of a Father: Forgiving the Unforgivable *(New Hope Publishers), which is currently being made into a movie, visit www.KittyChappell.com.*

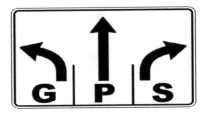

Lost? Try GPS
(God's Positioning System)

For God so loved the world that he gave his one and only Son, that whoever believes in him shall not perish but have eternal life.

JOHN 3:16

STUPID STUFF I'VE DONE

ANITA HIGMAN

When I was a kid, my grandfather gave my brother and me a shoebox of gunpowder, since my brother was so talented at making homemade fireworks. (I know. It's still a pretty bizarre present to give two mischievous kids, but let's not go there.) We thought it might be entertaining to toss some of the explosive into an open fire. So we started throwing bits of the volatile substance into a small bonfire we'd created in the backyard. The display of sparkles and fizz was spectacular. We'd created our own light show!

If you're wondering where my parents were, remember, this was back in the days when bad things rarely happened to kids. Parents, therefore, didn't supervise as closely as we do today. Apparently my brother and I were determined to blow that concept right out of the water.

Little did we realize that each time we threw a handful of gunpowder into the fire, some of the fine particles of the explosive drizzled out, creating a perfect fuse from the box of gunpowder to the fire. Need I say more? As we stood there watching the fire, a sudden, deafening explosion racked my body. The impact didn't strike my brother as fiercely, but I flew right over a high fence—landing on my head in some shrubbery.

When my father found me, my eyes were crossed. He had tears in his eyes and a look of despair on his face, and I was terrified. Thank God, my eyes later returned to normal. I'm sure I smelled like scorched chicken feathers. I remember feeling trapped in some kind of surreal daze for hours, but I realize now the accident could have been so much worse. I could have easily lost my sight—or even my life. I wish I could say that in my years on this planet that was my single act of stupidity. But I've actually amassed quite an impressive repertoire of such foolhardy choices, including many spiritual failings. One of the most painful was helping to put my ailing mother in a nursing home. My father was no longer able to care for my mother at home, but I still felt we could have tried to find a better alternative than placing her in the home. If I had listened to God and my mother, surely a more loving situation could have been arranged for the last months of her life. The hurried decision was no less than faithless folly, and I have since begged the Lord many times for forgiveness.

But he's a perfect Father, good and just, a gentle discipliner, and full of mercy, patience, encouragement, and loving-kindness. God has been faithful in forgiving a stupid sinner like me. So, this is my greeting card to the Almighty—filled with loving thanks for his commitment to me while I learn to follow him, and for loving me even when I'm foolish or when my faith falls flat.

I'm full of deep gratitude for his care and compassion through the years, whether it was over my recklessness or my sinful behavior. He was there with a watchful eye, loving and staying with me until I came to my senses. Or until I came to my knees.

Thank you, God. These are my simple words, from my grateful heart to heaven. With much love, from your Anita.

Award-winning author Anita Higman has seventeen books published as well as a novella and contributions in eight nonfiction compilations. Anita would love for you to visit her Web site at www.anitahigman.com.

L IS FOR LOSER?

One weekend last summer we had planned a fun family outing—but I felt miserable. It seemed I couldn't do anything right. No one made me feel this way except myself. I just felt vulnerable and sensitive and fat (it was swimsuit season, remember?) and … well, like a loser. This loser thing was going pretty deep. *How could God use me when I am such a mess?* I wondered. I felt condemned by wrong choices, and I felt lost in certain areas of my life. Then, the very next morning, my good buddy Ozzie (Oswald Chambers) had something to say about my situation. During my devotions, I read, "Oh, the bravery of God in trusting us! Do you say, 'But He has been unwise to choose me, because there is nothing good in me and I have no value'? That is exactly why He chose you" (*My Utmost For His Highest*, Oswald Chambers, August 4).

Wow. Ozzie goes on to explain that as long as we think we're hot stuff, God won't use us, because then we'll have our own agenda. Okay, let me say again, *wow*. God wants us empty, so *he* can fill us up. It's "not of what we bring with us, but of what God puts into us."

I've never liked it when people call each other "loser." I used to think, "No one is a loser."

But I've changed my way of thinking now. We are *all* losers. When we think we are winners, we become disappointed in ourselves because we don't always do everything right—like a winner would. Then we think we're not good enough for anyone, including God.

Don't get me wrong. God isn't asking us to go around feeling sorry for ourselves because we are "losers." Quite the opposite.

We may *all* be losers, but because we have Christ in our lives, we're going to be okay, warts and all. As long as we hold our arms open wide to him, asking *him* to fill us up, we *gotta* be okay—because we have the winner of all time on our side.

He loves us so much, he's picked us for his team. Imagine! L isn't for Loser, it's for Love.

SUPREME MAKEOVER

DENA DYER

Why am I so hard on myself?" I asked my hubby in the midst of a hormonal flood of tears. I felt frustrated (again) by my body's slow response to my efforts at losing the "baby weight" from my second child. "Why can't I accept where I am, do my best to be healthy, and leave it at that?!"

I knew Carey wasn't the culprit—in our ten plus years together, he has loved me through thick and thin (literally!). Part of the answer, I knew, stemmed from the pressure I felt from our culture—pressure to be svelte once again, no matter the cost.

You've seen the "reality" shows where real women get transformed—via plastic surgery, dental work, exercise, wardrobe changes, hair extensions, and extreme diets—into supermodels. You may have even wished you could be selected as a participant. I know I've been tempted once or twice to at least get my teeth whitened again or pay for one of those really expensive, really restrictive diet plans.

But lately, I've been repulsed by the snatches of makeovers I've seen while my husband flicks between channels. Why?

Well, I've discovered that the ladies (not so much the men, who retain some semblance of their former selves) all come out looking alike. Creepily, Stepfordian-alike. Yikes. What have we become?

Several things have happened lately to solidify my disgust at the way the current culture (especially the popular media) makes women loathe our bodies. No news flash here: We are an appearance-driven, celebrity-obsessed, beauty-addicted society.

First, I noticed how, two months after giving birth, a fellow mother at our local moms' support group looked beautiful but felt horrible about herself because none of her clothes fit. After I told her how pretty she looked, she sighed, grimaced, and said, "Ugh. I've gotta lose weight."

For the first time, I saw how I'd been reacting to my sweet hubby when he complimented me. I also realized how ridiculous it is that we expect ourselves, and even other women, to "bounce back" from childbirth right into exercise, a healthy diet, and then—way too soon to be realistic—our pre-pregnancy clothes. We look at Reese Witherspoon, Julia Roberts, and Kate Hudson—who reportedly squeeze back into their pre-baby wardrobes in eight weeks—and think, "Why can't I do that?" Well, it's because they have to lose weight or they'll lose their jobs.

How would you like that pressure, besides being sleep-deprived, hormonal, and sore? Those gals spend literally hours a day at the gym (*not* with their precious newborns) so that they can continue their careers. I'm sorry, but to me, that's not a real life.

The second experience that transformed my mind-set occurred when I read a story in a fashion magazine. In the article, a woman who has had cancer—and is in remission—wrote about an upcoming fitting for a bridesmaid dress. She admitted that if she hadn't lost ten pounds before the appointment, she'd rather go to a biopsy! Later in that same piece, her sister (who was undergoing treatment for a different type of cancer) raved about how she had lost ten pounds for that same wedding—through chemotherapy. Whoa.

I wonder, has cancer made them more compassionate, more sure of their purpose? Has it made them treasure life in all its glorious fragility? I sure hope so. *Those* would be the benefits worth exulting in—not weight loss.

Bottom line: We are a sad, sick, self-absorbed society. Even Christians have fallen for the lie that what you look like determines your value. And I have been part of it for way too long. But *no more!*

Ladies, this is what I believe—finally, really, truly believe: I am beautiful. And so are you. So is every person on this planet. We are made in God's image, and we are loved by our heavenly Father as his glorious children. I look at my kids and I don't see anything but absolute perfection and awe-inspiring beauty. Why do we think God sees us any differently?! The Scriptures teach us that when God looks at us, he sees us through the filter of Jesus—the lens of grace.

Don't get me wrong: I'm not, by any means, knocking nutrition and fitness. I definitely believe we need to take care of ourselves, because, as the Bible reminds us, we're the temple of God. Why wouldn't we want to treat our Father's house with respect? I've just come to believe that respect goes both ways. Just as we should exercise to build and maintain strength, and take in healthy food and drink to give our bodies fuel, we also shouldn't beat up on ourselves for becoming more wrinkled, hippy, or heavy as we age.

Whether we're smooth, wizened, jiggly, firm, tan, or pale, we are all beautiful. And we are so much more than what shows on the outside. After all, the most gorgeous women I know are stunning simply because they know who they are—and who loves them.

Now, if I can keep that belief front-and-center while the culture waves its "you must be perfect to be loved/successful/beautiful" flag all around me, I'll have achieved something worthwhile.

Pardon me, will you? I'm going to go cancel my subscription to a certain magazine.

STARSHINE'S SMILE MARKERS

Part of honoring him is honoring our children and husband. Instead of lamenting flabby arms today, rejoice that those arms embrace the people God has placed in your life. Rejoice that he made you just as you are—to house the Holy Spirit and to bring hope to that large segment of the world that's dying under the strain of having to be beautiful to be loved.

MARY DEMUTH

ORDINARY MOM, EXTRAORDINARY GOD (HARVEST HOUSE)

WATCH YOUR STEP

RHONDA RHEA

I was wearing exceptionally cute shoes. (Somehow it's important to note that.) Cute shoes are so integral to a classy look. The problem with cute shoes, however, is that they're so seldom practical. I don't remember anyone ever saying to me, "Take a look at my adorable orthopedic shoes!" Nope, cute usually means painful. Sometimes it even means dangerous.

Case in point: the Sunday night I sported the exceptionally cute shoes. While fashion-consciously walking down the runway ... er ... *hallway* at church, one of the attractive high heels made an unexpected forty-five-degree turn to the west. The rest of me took on a new course, heading due east. Maybe if it had been a few degrees less, I could've pulled out at the last minute. Instinctively, I concluded that forty-five degrees is past the point of no return. I was going down. Mayday!

Go ahead. Try to hang on to your graceful, charming look while taking a nose dive in the middle of the church hallway. In a dress. I tried to bounce up with an "I *so* meant to do that," but no one bought it.

Fortunately, as we were between rush hours in the church hall, I only humiliated myself in front of a handful of people. I have to give them credit. They tried hard to look sincerely concerned—right before exploding into uncontrolled laughter. I thought I might have to give one of them a little CPR. I hate it when I make my friends swallow their gum.

By the way, it doesn't matter how cute the shoes are, they just don't give you that runway look when they end up flying through the air. We just never know when life can take a bad, unexpected turn. Ephesians 5:15–17 says, "So watch your step. Use your head. Make the most of every chance you get. These are desperate times! Don't live carelessly, unthinkingly. Make sure you understand what the Master wants" (MSG). God wants us to use our time wisely, loving him and loving others.

Watching our step doesn't necessarily mean always wearing sensible shoes. But it does mean we need to guard our thinking and our actions. Spending too much time on a "look" is not making the most of every opportunity to live for Christ. Living carelessly and unthinkingly is dangerous. We need to forget the runway and "understand what the Master wants."

We find what he wants spelled out plainly for us in his Word. The love directions in the Word of God will never send us spiraling out of control. No unexpected west turns there! It's the safe and secure life. The life of love. The clean life. Psalm 119:9 says, "How can a young person live a clean life? By carefully reading the map of your Word" (MSG).

If you've been spiraling out of control or quietly heading down the wrong kind of runway, it's time to dust yourself off and change directions. Head God-ward. Follow his map for loving and living. There's joy there. Even in orthopedic shoes.

Rhonda Rhea is a speaker, radio personality, humor columnist, and the author of several books, including Amusing Grace *(Cook Communications) and* Who Put the Cat in the Fridge? Serving Up Hope and Hilarity Family Style *(Cook Communications). Visit www.RhondaRhea.net.*

STARSHINE'S HOW'S YOUR INNERSTATE?

Is It Really Reality?

While reading Proverbs (*The Message*), I thought about the so-called reality shows that are so popular right now. Solomon, the author of Proverbs, recorded some really practical advice, much of which applies to reality television participants—and those of us who regularly find ourselves drawn in (I can attest—they *are* addictive!).

He might ask the men and women who populate the dating shows: "Why would you trade intimacies for dalliance with a promiscuous stranger?" I can imagine him questioning the scores of people who offer themselves up for "beauty pageants" and over-the-top makeovers: "Why should you allow strangers to take advantage of you? Why be exploited by those who care nothing for you?" Perhaps he'd even give this advice to pop and movie star wannabe's: "Easy come, easy go—but steady diligence pays off."

What would he say to cast members of the shows that honor deceit and manipulation instead of honesty and integrity? Maybe, "Truth lasts; lies are here today, gone tomorrow" or "Evil scheming distorts the schemer; peace-planning brings joy to the planner."

Solomon would surely tell *Fear Factor* folks: "The fear of God is a spring of living water so you won't go off drinking from poisoned wells," and "The fear of human opinion disables; trusting in God protects you from that."

And though *Big Brother* is hardly worth mentioning, Solomon might tell the housemates, "The more talk, the less truth; the wise measure their words," or "Mean-spirited slander is heartless; quiet discretion accompanies good sense."

(Hmmm … discretion. A lost word in this age of "letting it all hang out"—sometimes literally—in front of millions of viewers.)

Don't let anyone tell you the Bible isn't relevant in today's world. Listen how well this quote applies to *Survivor* contestants: "If you think you know it all, you're a fool for sure; real survivors learn wisdom from others."

I also like these verses: "Don't figure ways of taking advantage of a neighbor when he's sitting there trusting and unsuspecting" and "Make your motions and cast your votes, but God has the final say."

And here's my favorite: "Isn't it obvious that conspirators lose out, while the thoughtful win love and trust?"

While it may not be obvious on television, it *will* be clear one day. And whether the world believes it or not, that's reality.

Love vs. the Soup Ladle

Barbara Tripp

I never saw her actually hit anyone when she threatened us with her soup ladle. Her harsh voice and the spoon raised high above her head were enough to keep us in a state of fear.

In 1975, while in my mid-twenties, my husband and I went through a difficult time in our relationship. We lost our home and careers and very nearly lost our marriage. Then God stepped in and stirred up our lives. We found ourselves in a small town, strangers looking for work.

They say hindsight is 20/20. I should have known something was up by the sight of the faded and dusty "help wanted" sign. It looked as if it sat in the bakery window permanently.

Sure enough, I got the job the same day I applied. Threats, shouting, swearing, and name-calling filled my first day of work. Among the employees, there was no talking, no joking or smiling.

So when I got home after my first day of work, I fell on my knees and asked God, *what have I gotten myself into?* All night I wrestled with the desire to quit. In the morning, I felt like God had given me a one-word answer: love. He had changed my life with his love; now I needed to demonstrate his love to my boss. But she just happened to be as unlovable a person as I'd ever met.

That morning I arrived at work, smiled at her, and wished her a good morning. Suddenly, all eyes were on the two of us. No one ever greeted her that way. No one dared to greet *anyone* that way.

She responded by raising the soup ladle and screaming, "Get to work."

All day I persisted in looking for ways to be helpful, considerate, and kind, not only to her but also to my fellow employees.

Days passed with no change, and I wanted to give up. But I persisted, and eventually I began to notice a difference, not in her—but in my coworkers. After a week, we all began greeting each other with smiles and good mornings. The one person of color, who had been treated no better than a slave, started to hold his head up. On breaks, he and I talked about his life's goal, which was to get a college education. By year's end, he was accepted at a university.

Another young man there was a very good artist, but no one knew it. The boss disrespected him and insulted him any way she could. As one of his duties, he wrote the day's menu on a chalkboard and placed it on the sidewalk. I encouraged him to add some art.

"I'll get in trouble," he said. But he decorated the chalkboard anyway and it was an instant success. As it happened, one of our customers was the editor of the local newspaper. He was so impressed that he soon hired the young man to illustrate political cartoons for the editorial page.

After a few months, even my boss began to thaw. First, she started exchanging greetings with her employees. Then she actually used the soup ladle for its intended purpose instead of berating the workers. Swear words only popped out of her mouth when she was exasperated. She began to smile, and finally, if we did a good job, she told us so.

So if you find yourself in a difficult work environment and can't (or don't want to) quit, try dishing out a healthy portion of God's love mixed with a dash of patience. Then sit back and expect a miracle.

Barbara Tripp is a joyful and active grandmother and has written articles for Family Tree Magazine, Positive Teen Magazine, Women's Independent Press, The Orlando Sentinel, *and several e-zines.*

STARSHINE'S SMILE MARKERS

Does the neutral onlooker identify a Christian by his pious practices and cultic regularity or by the loving quality of his everyday presence in the workaday world?

BRENNAN MANNING

A GLIMPSE OF JESUS

(HARPERCOLLINS)

PILOT'S HALO

MIRANDA ROBERTS

The air was gray and foggy as we left Dallas and headed to Omaha. Outside the plane's window, nothing showed but white. Occasionally, a bit of denser cloud floated by, but except for that, there was no indication that we were moving at all. Fuzzy, wrinkled whiteness spread out like so much unrolled cotton candy, and I couldn't see anything on the ground to distinguish where I was or where I was headed.

It was a perfect analogy of my life. Faced with a marital separation, financial struggles, concerns on a number of levels for my nearly grown boys, and the inevitable angst about my own future, I felt just as disoriented.

Now, on this twenty-eight-hour whirlwind trip to Dallas, I was helping my brother and sister-in-law add hospice care to my dad's nursing home care.

When we landed, a dear friend met my plane. As she was in the midst of her own difficult season, we'd become a lifeline for each other. Often, we'd talked about how God can see above the mist and knows whether or not we're going in the right direction. We'd been trying to hone our spiritual ears to listen for his voice as we made our way through our respective fogs so that we would come out on the other side having learned whatever he wanted to teach us. We'd also prayed to become more conformed to his likeness. So before my brother came to take me to see our Dad, my friend and I spent a couple of hours together, talking and encouraging one another.

Dad's nursing home, it turned out, was more of an assisted-living house. Situated in a residential area, the place housed three clients and one full-time caregiver. I liked the homey atmosphere instantly and liked the fact that it was close enough to my brother's home that he and his family visited regularly. They developed relationships with the other residents and knew Dad was in good hands.

Thankfully, Dad knew me and was glad to see me. But he'd recently been hospitalized, and his health had declined significantly since the last time I had seen him. He didn't track with our conversations very well and seemed confused and vague. Since it was evening by then and he was tired, we didn't stay long before returning to my brother's house.

Later that evening, my brother, a pilot for a major airline as well as an amateur photographer, showed me some of the photos he had taken from the cockpit of the planes he had flown. I saw stunning pictures of glaciers in Iceland, sunrises and sunsets, and other planes as they passed above or beneath his. One picture in particular caught my attention, though. It was a picture of clouds, and right in front, a perfectly formed, circular rainbow.

"Pilot's Halo," he told me. "That's what we call it, anyway. It has to do with the light bending around the airplane and refracting the light in the clouds to form the halo."

The light in that picture was so bright that a second, fainter halo had formed around the first. That outer, fainter rainbow took the colors in reverse order of the inner one. It was absolutely beautiful.

The next morning we returned to see Dad, who was now having a difficult time. His caregiver had been able to get him to the breakfast table with the aid of his walker, but when he wanted to return to his room, his legs couldn't hold him. Wheeling him back, it seemed he was in pain but couldn't tell us where he hurt.

Seeing him in pain and knowing I couldn't stay and spend time with him distressed me. It tore me up to see him so changed from the last time I had been there, just a few short months ago—and so changed from the man he used to be.

I barely had a chance to meet the hospice nurse. Our meeting was about as routine as I'd expected. She seemed competent and answered all our questions patiently and thoroughly. But before she started her initial assessment of Dad, I had to leave to catch my plane. I felt disappointed to miss such an important step and saddened that my time there had passed so quickly. And I felt guilty.

Dad had changed so quickly. Would this be the last time I could talk to him and have him understand me, at least on some level? I'd had so little time with him on this visit; I didn't want to leave him. Airline schedules are unyielding, however, and my plane was scheduled to get me home just in time to pick up my youngest son from school. I had no choice but to say good-bye to Dad and head to the airport.

Sitting on the plane, feeling sad and burdened, I reflected on the last twenty-four hours. Both of my brothers had strong marriages and spouses who were there for them to help them through the days ahead. I didn't have that. I was leaving uncertainty behind me in Dallas, and I was coming home to uncertainty as well. Despite those thoughts, I prayed and tried to remind myself of what I'd been reading in a book: The things of earth really do pale compared to the reality of Jesus' love.

Outside my window, I saw a seemingly endless cloud cover. Just like on the first flight, I couldn't distinguish anything familiar on the ground. I could barely even tell we were moving. I'd just have to trust that the pilot knew where we were going and how to get us there. Closing my eyes, I reminded myself that's what my life had been—trusting Jesus, my life's pilot, to direct my path and get me to the destination he had mapped out for me.

When I opened my eyes and glanced out the window again, I noticed something wonderful. There against the clouds below and slightly ahead of the plane, was a Pilot's Halo! That perfectly round rainbow had seemingly been put there just for me. The rainbow was a symbol of his faithfulness and the circle, a symbol of eternity. Together, they created a reminder to trust. I knew, suddenly, that I wasn't alone. I wasn't unsupported. God's eternal faithfulness had manifested itself right outside my window.

The Halo stayed with us for the rest of the trip. As we began our descent into Omaha, and the plane approached the top of the cloud cover, the circle seemed to grow larger. It was then that I noticed the most wonderful part of it all. As we reached the top of the clouds, the shadow of the plane appeared in the center of the Halo.

There I was, in my comparatively little airplane, surrounded by the all-encompassing faithfulness of God. My heart filled with gratitude and my eyes filled with tears as I thanked God for this precious gift.

As we neared the top of the clouds, the shadow of the plane loomed ever larger, but the Halo could still be seen, as if on the other side of it. Sometimes life looms so large it's hard to see God's faithfulness, but he is still there—regardless.

Finally, we entered the clouds, and the plane's shadow and its accompanying halo were lost to my view. But they weren't lost to my memory.

I got off the plane with no change in my circumstances. My marriage and my finances were still precarious. I still had all the responsibilities, questions, and uncertainties I had when I had gotten on the plane. And I still had to scramble out to my car in order to get to my son's school to pick him up on time.

Though my problems remained, my heart had been lightened. I had been reminded in a personal, tangible way that nothing is bigger than God. No problem. No enemy. No circumstance. His love and faithfulness surround me—always.

Miranda Roberts is the pseudonym for a groovy chick who received her love of words from both of her parents. Her mother was a poet and a wonderful letter-writer; both of her parents were avid readers. They are both gone now, but their love of words lives on in Miranda's brothers and in herself.

STARSHINE'S SMILE MARKERS

Feelings of guilt, accompanied by anxiety, fear and restlessness, arise from deep within ourselves and are not an accurate gauge of the state of our souls before God. We cannot assume that he feels about us the way we feel about ourselves, unless we love ourselves intensely and freely.

BERNARD BUSH

FROM AN ESSAY "COPING WITH GOD" (QUOTED IN BRENNAN MANNING'S *A GLIMPSE OF JESUS*, HarperCollins, 2003)

FIVE GROOVY WAYS TO SAY "I LOVE YOU" TO GOD

PEPPER'S PIT STOPS

1. Discover your *Sacred Pathway*, a thoughtful book by Gary Thomas. Make a point of worshipping God in the way he made you.

2. Write letters or songs to him.

3. Be his missionary by living a godly life every day, everywhere you live.

4. Pray, then listen. Write down distracting thoughts and clear your head. Wait for his voice.

5. Learn to see yourself the way God sees you.

THE CAT RUG

BETH A. ORTSTADT

I always knew, in the back of my mind, that it wouldn't be a good idea for my husband and me to build a house together. It became crystal clear in the last several months. After over a decade of marriage, we decided it was time to get rid of all of the "premarital" furniture that was crowding our basement. The grouping included his huge bachelor couch that swallowed you up as you watched television, along with the matching man-recliner, of course. And then there was my bachelorette sofa and love seat with the decidedly '80s color scheme. We both agreed it was time for these pieces to go.

With all the kids potty-trained, we even felt brave enough to consider splurging on some high-end stuff. The challenge came in mutually deciding what this "stuff" would be.

Several months of furniture shopping ensued. We must have visited every reasonable furniture store in our metropolitan area, and at least one in a neighboring county, not to mention conducting Internet searches for distant furniture stores. It got to the point where the mere mention of the word "furniture" drove our children into hiding, for fear that they would find themselves in another store full of couches they couldn't sit on.

I'm not convinced that furniture shopping should be a coed activity. My husband and I have different approaches, not to mention different tastes, when it comes to home decorating. My approach is to settle on a master plan, a style, a theme that harmonizes the individual pieces, and I obsess over whether we might be breaking some nebulous decorating rules. My husband's philosophy, on the other hand, is "If I like two things, then they go together."

I have an admitted weakness for getting too close to designers and decorators. I fear hurting their feelings if I don't take their suggestions or buy their overpriced couches. I don't think I even need to say where my left-brain, engineer husband stands on this issue. ("Decorators, schmecorators.")

I regularly clear off the refrigerator door (stashing away all the miscellaneous magnets and papers which have accumulated on it) to achieve a streamlined, magazine page look. He comes home and says, "It looks like nobody lives here."

My greatest surprise, when we bought our first home, was that he would even have an opinion about home decor. I thought that I'd just decorate the house and he'd say, "That's fine, honey." I suppose the fact that he actually had opinions about the wedding should have tipped me off. (I won't go into details about the tie and cummerbund he selected, inspired by his college colors.)

My first wake-up call to compromise in home decorating was the cat rug. I'm not talking about a rug where the cat sleeps. This is a large latch hook rug that prominently features a Siamese cat. It showed up in the hallway of our first home shortly after we moved in. The cat rug came to be a sort of shibboleth between his people and my people. You either "got" the cat rug or you didn't.

And I and my people—we didn't get it.

In my defense, my only encounter with latch hook prior to marriage was when my sister had an extended stay in a psychiatric hospital. She was given a latch hook project as one form of occupational therapy.

In my husband's family, there is a bastion of latch hook tradition. His beloved grandmother had a black belt in latch hook. She single-handedly created enough pieces to leave at least one to every member in the extended family. And her influence moved other family members to dabble in latch hook too. In fact, my husband's first latch hook rug survives to this day and graces the floor of our daughter's room. And at this very moment, my daughter is sitting at her dad's feet with her very own latch hook.

Also in my defense, I never kept a cat long enough to grow attached. The few animals we ever had in our home either ran away or threw themselves in front of moving cars (except for the turtles, who threw themselves under Dad's lawn mower).

My husband's family had a Siamese cat for nearly eighteen years, and her importance to the family is clear. She's the subject of more home movie footage than some of her human "siblings."

Not long after we settled into our new home, some of my college friends came for a visit. The first item on the agenda was a tour of the house. "What's with the cat rug?" one of them asked, with all the tact of a really close friend.

I tried to explain my in-laws' latch hooking tradition and their beloved Siamese cat. "But why do you have to have it in your hall?"

Obviously she wasn't married yet. Love means having a cat rug on your floor, even if you don't see how it fits into the overall decorating scheme. Love means hanging an antique Spanish sword on the wall and a dartboard in the family room. It means dedicating a whole bookcase to baseball card storage. For my husband, love means living with a flowered bedspread, fruity wallpaper in the dining room, and an abundance of fake ivy scattered around the house.

Not everything in our house matches. Not everything is neat and tidy. None of our rooms would make the pages of any decorating magazine. But they are filled with the give-and-take of over a decade of shared living, with memories we have built together.

The things in my home are daily reminders that it's really not about me. Each time I glance at something that is more my husband's taste than mine, I'm reminded again of the surrender that love requires. And it is often the small, tangible things that are hardest to surrender. I can easily promise my faithfulness until death do us part, but I'm not so eager to agree on the thermostat setting and the direction the toilet paper should be rolled. I will love him and cherish him, but I'd rather not give him any say on paint colors.

It occurs to me that the same is true in my relationship to God. It is easy to offer him my heart, but I'd like to hang on to some of my favorite bad habits. He can build the house of my life, but I'd like to decorate it to my own taste, thank you very much.

I will worship him and spend time in his Word and even teach Sunday school. But let me nurse my anger and resentment when a sick child keeps me trapped at home for a week. Let me buy that blouse that makes me feel younger and sexier, even if it isn't particularly modest. Let me watch some trashy television, since I know what they're doing is wrong, and I just want to see what they're wearing, anyway.

It is no surprise that Christ compares our relationship to him with marriage. Learning to let go of the little things out of love for my husband is good practice. It is practice in letting go of every little piece of my life to God. It's a reminder to let God decorate my spiritual house to his taste. I may wince at some of the things he chooses or pout about giving up something I would rather have, but in the end, love means surrender.

So maybe it's not a good idea for us ever to build a house together, but we are building a home marked by love—and a lot of white flags.

Beth A. Ortstadt "retired" from professional ministry to take on the challenges of full-time motherhood. She makes her not-so-perfect home in Wichita, Kansas, with her husband, two kids, and six to eight fish (depending on the week).

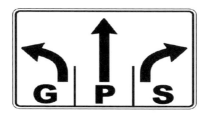

Lost? Try GPS
(God's Positioning System)

If I speak in the tongues of men and of angels, but have not love, I am only a resounding gong or a clanging cymbal. If I have the gift of prophecy and can fathom all mysteries and all knowledge, and if I have a faith that can move mountains, but have not love, I am nothing. If I give all I possess to the poor and surrender my body to the flames, but have not love, I gain nothing.

Love is patient, love is kind. It does not envy, it does not boast, it is not proud. It is not rude, it is not self-seeking, it is not easily angered, it keeps no record of wrongs. Love does not delight in evil but rejoices with the truth. It always protects, always trusts, always hopes, always perseveres.

Love never fails. But where there are prophecies, they will cease; where there are tongues, they will be stilled; where there is knowledge, it will pass away. For we know in part and we prophesy in part, but when perfection comes, the imperfect disappears. When I was a child, I talked like a child, I thought like a child, I reasoned like a child. When I became a man, I put childish ways behind me. Now we see but a poor reflection as in a mirror; then we shall see face to face. Now I know in part; then I shall know fully, even as I am fully known.

And now these three remain: faith, hope and love. But the greatest of these is love.

1 CORINTHIANS 13

STARSHINE'S SMILE MARKERS

Life with Christ is endless love;
without Him it is a loveless end.
BILLY GRAHAM
HOPE FOR THE TROUBLED HEART
(W PUBLISHING)

So You Wanna Be a Groovy Chick, Too?

H ere are a few ways to let your inner GC shine—and find other friends who will support your GC lifestyle.

☺ Come up with your own Groovy Chick Chapter and tell us what you are doing. We will put the winner on our Web site (http://groovychicksroadtrip.com), and we may even include your idea in our next book! Give us your idea by clicking on "Write-a-Chick."

☺ Look for bargains on lava lamps, door beads, and cute kitschy stuff at Target, Ross, T.J. Maxx, Marshall's, and other discount stores. Then find a corner of your home and/or office to decorate—and dedicate—as your own GC corner of the universe. Soon, it will attract other gals who are just waiting for permission to be groovy!

☺ Buy "chick lit" novels like *She's All That* by Kristin Billerbeck (Integrity, 2005) or *Sisterchicks Say Ooh La La!* by Robin Jones Gunn (Multnomah, 2005) at your local Christian bookstore. Then savor them, slowly, while 1) sitting on your sunporch and drinking iced tea, 2) lounging in bed and sipping hot cocoa, or 3) chilling at Starbucks and slurping a cool mocha cappuccino.

☺ Gather friends to go bargain hunting for "groovy get-ups" at the Goodwill store, Salvation Army, or your local retro/resale shop. When you find the right combination of clothes and accessories, put the outfits on and drive through town (preferably NOT in your minivan), belting out 60's tunes while other drivers stare in awe (no, that's NOT horror registering on their faces—it's awe!).

☺ Plan a road trip with your girlfriends or family members, using the hints in *Pepper's Pit Stops* to get your ideas flowing. If you can "get your kicks" while driving on the REAL Route 66, even better! Send us pics!

☺ For a low-cost alternative to a road trip, plan an at-home evening or slumber party. Rent chick flicks, have your friends bring snacks, and give each other beauty treatments. Create a theme, such as "Hope Floats" (decorate with balloons, make ice cream floats, and watch the movie—the one with Sandra Bullock and groovy cutie, Harry Connick Jr.) or "Bed and Breakfast" (bring mattresses and pillows into the living room to lounge on, watch *Breakfast at Tiffany's*, and make pancakes to nosh on).

☺ Plan a comedy night at your church and invite all your churchless friends. They might want to be groovy in God, too!

☺ As you find your groove, remember to share the contagious joy of being God's gal! Tell others you're Groovy only through Christ's love.

Thanks for taking this road trip with us. Be on the lookout for other Groovy Chick books, and above all, remember—Jesus loves you, *just the way you are.* Now *that's* Groovy!

—Pepper and Starshine (Laurie and Dena)